D1715317

Crosscurrents / MODERN CRITIQUES

Harry T. Moore, *General Editor*

The Fiction of KATHERINE MANSFIELD

Marvin Magalaner

WITH A PREFACE BY

Harry T. Moore

SOUTHERN ILLINOIS UNIVERSITY PRESS
Carbondale and Edwardsville

FEFFER & SIMONS, INC.
London and Amsterdam

To Seth, Jillian, and Darcy

Printed in the United States of America
Designed by Andor Braun
ISBN 0-8093-0478-3
Library of Congress Catalog Card Number 74-132489

Contents

Preface

As everyone knows, Poe, de Maupassant, and Chekhov made the short story (earlier so neatly used for ancient legends and in Boccaccio's Decameron*) into an important modern literary form. A subsequent writer, during and just after the First World War, wrote a number of stories which still glow with life: Katherine Mansfield, who died in 1923 at the age of thirty-four. She produced voluminously in that short lifetime, as the posthumously published letters, journals, and reviews show.*

A great admirer of Chekhov, she manifested something of his quality in her tales, with their occasional lack of consecutiveness and with their tendency to dramatize through understatement. But she didn't in any important way imitate Chekhov, any more than she imitated the French symboliste *writers when she wrote in a somewhat symbolistic vein. No, her vision was her own; if often narrow, it sometimes went deep. But as her onetime friend D. H. Lawrence wrote to her former husband, John Middleton Murry, after her death, her work could not really be called "great."*

Yet it has persisted, and it continues to charm readers today, usually those with a sensitivity to character development through sudden flashes of insight and to an author capable of using language vividly. Brought up in New Zealand, Katherine Mansfield was accustomed to seeing phenomena as if in sharp outline, brightened by the southern sun.

In the present book, Professor Marvin Magalaner of the City University of New York—who has done such fine and important work on Joyce—discusses Katherine Mansfield's outstanding stories. Taking a limited number of them in this way, he can deal with each of them at some length, showing their relevance to the rest of this author's work. He provides valuable new interpretations of these stories, when necessary drawing upon biography, as in his analysis of "Something Childish But Very Natural," whose "idyllic love affair involving two children" reflects the author's association with Middleton Murry. In discussing this and other notable Mansfield stories—"Prelude," "The Bay," "Bliss," "The Garden Party," and others—Mr. Magalaner deals especially with technique, psychology, language, and theme. He furnishes an excellent prelude of his own by making his opening chapter an overview of Katherine Mansfield as a critic.

By calling her plain Mansfield, he solves one difficulty in dealing with her. The name of the subject always presents an acute problem for any author of a book—criticism or biography—which focuses upon one central figure: what to call him or her. A few years ago, the F. Scott Fitzgeralds' daughter complained in print that too many people who hadn't known her parents would blithely write of them as Scott and Zelda. Of course one can always say Fitzgerald, though the name is rather long; in referring to Middleton Murry and Katherine Mansfield, I have sometimes written of them as Murry and Katherine—I didn't know Katherine Mansfield, and yet couldn't go on using her full name. And Miss Mansfield seems a little stiff and awkward. But Mr. Magalaner has solved this and similar difficulties in the present book by taking courses of action that can only be called wise.

HARRY T. MOORE

Southern Illinois University
November 11, 1970

Acknowledgments

Grateful acknowledgment for permission to reprint from the following works of Katherine Mansfield is extended to the publishers: Alfred A. Knopf, Inc. for permission to quote from *The Aloe, The Journal of Katherine Mansfield, Katherine Mansfield's Letters to John Middleton Murry: 1913–1922, The Letters of Katherine Mansfield, The Scrapbook of Katherine Mansfield, The Short Stories of Katherine Mansfield*, and *Novels & Novelists;* Beacon Press for quotation from their paperback edition of *Novels & Novelists;* and to the Society of Authors for quotation from the works of Katherine Mansfield which it controls.

The Fiction of Katherine Mansfield

1

The Enigma of Katherine Mansfield

Almost a half century after her death, Katherine Mansfield still eludes easy summing up. The "fiendish . . . polecat" of Beatrice Hastings's memories is a far cry from the ultrafastidious bohemian artist of Antony Alpers's biography.[1] Even to her husband, John Middleton Murry, Mansfield seems difficult to classify. The strong-willed woman, the unrelenting artist, the aggressive partner often give way to the cranky patient, the babyish child-wife, the maddeningly unreasonable female.

The blurred outlines cannot be blamed on lack of available evidence either. Few "minor" literary figures have accumulated after their death the sheer bulk of evaluative materials that now constitute the Mansfield canon—much of it carefully edited by her late husband ostensibly to bring the picture into proper focus. Two imposing volumes of letters, one *Scrapbook*, one *Journal*, one biography coauthored by Murry, explanatory prefaces to most of the editions of her stories by Murry, and numerous volumes of autobiography and memoir by Murry in which the emphasis is on Mansfield as wife, companion, artist, offer to the reader a bewilderingly volatile person whose principal characteristic appears to be inconsistency in personal affairs. Nor do biographical works by detached outsiders like Antony Alpers help much to sharpen Mansfield's image.[2]

One may suggest, of course, that the blurred impression of inconsistency that these writings produce is the truth about the person called Katherine Mansfield rather than a defect in observation or recording on the part of the writers. Mansfield herself is recorded as saying that maybe "there are people whose reality is cut up into such a number of little fragments that they can't find it themselves," people, that is, "who are different every time you see them." [3] And though she seems not to be thinking of herself in the context of this specific statement, there are many points in her autobiographical writing and in her stories at which she recognizes the psychological necessity of the mask. To Murry she writes:

It's a terrible thing to be alone. Yes, it is—it is. But don't lower your mask until you have another mask prepared beneath—as terrible as you like—but a mask.[4]

In another letter, she confides to him that she "dare not keep a journal. I should always be trying to tell the truth. As a matter of fact I dare not tell the truth. I feel I *must* not. The only way to exist is to go on and try and lose oneself." [5] Awareness of the horror of Katherine Mansfield's life makes it difficult to deny her whatever comfort masks and oblivion might afford.

Her childhood was perhaps the only period of her life that she could contemplate with any real pleasure. She was born in Wellington, New Zealand, in 1888 to upper middle-class parents, and spent her childhood in comfortable circumstances with her sisters and a brother.[6] Kathleen Beauchamp (her real name) was close to her mother (who plays a major role in "Prelude" and many other stories) but had mixed feelings regarding her father Harold Beauchamp, the town banker and a successful merchant.

When she was fifteen, her father sent her to Queen's

College in London, where she wrote sketches for the college literary periodical and got a taste of cosmopolitan cultural life that provincial New Zealand obviously could not match. Forced to return to Wellington in 1906, upon completing her school work, she found the old way of life totally unsuitable. By 1908, her will prevailed, and she was allowed to return to London to live and write, subsidized by a small allowance from her father.

Still in her teens, her willing introduction into the adult world of bohemia was sudden and brutal. In 1909, she married George Bowden and left him, disillusioned, in less than twenty-four hours. Shortly afterward she was pregnant by another man. The pregnancy resulted in a miscarriage which she endured in solitary anguish in a German retreat. Ill health dogged her during the next year and a serious operation disturbed her peace of mind. In 1911, ill health persisted, complicated by another affair that resulted in an abortion.

Nineteen twelve was the year in which she met John Middleton Murry, with whom she lived on and off until their marriage in 1918 when her divorce from George Bowden became final. During 1912, she continued to publish fiction in the *New Age* and began to write for Murry's *Rhythm* and the *Blue Review*. The war put an end to Murry's journals in 1914 but the new *Signature* provided a temporary outlet for Mansfield's art. In 1915, she suffered a serious blow with the death in France of her younger brother, Leslie Beauchamp. His death hastened her decision to write about their homeland and their childhood in New Zealand—the subject matter of "Prelude" and "At the Bay."

By 1916, Mansfield was a semi-invalid and was to remain so until her death seven years later. Because she had tuberculosis and heart trouble, the English climate was out of the question for her. Therefore she spent most of the period in France or Italy, mainly on the

Riviera. But while this treatment may have been indicated for her physical condition, the enforced absence from home and husband which it entailed—the impossibility of her putting roots down anywhere in the world—brought emotional and psychological maladies as awful as the diseases themselves.

From 1918 through 1922, she wrote most of her most distinguished fiction, though it was the period of her deepest sickness. "Prelude" was published in 1918, and in 1919 her husband assumed the editorshop of the *Athenaeum*, which provided a new and influential outlet for her criticism, fiction, and poetry. The periodical also carried translations by Mansfield and S. S. Koteliansky of a selection of the letters of Chekhov. Despairing of her life, Mansfield tried a series of radical cures for tuberculosis in 1922, eventually entering the Gurdjieff Institute near Paris. There, though she apparently improved psychologically to the point where visitors ordinarily describe her as "radiant," her physical condition grew increasingly worse. She died during a visit from John Middleton Murry on January 9, 1923.

These few paragraphs of chronology scarcely convey the accumulated horror of Mansfield's sick and lonely existence. Far more eloquent are the hundreds of letters which she wrote detailing the day-by-day, night-by-night tormnts that she endured, often phrased in the chirpy, forced gaiety of the chronic sufferer. The reader of these letters no longer wonders that Mansfield found it necessary to lose herself or to fragment her personality.

But Mansfield's legacy is neither her life nor her myth. It is the several hundred pages of fiction that still compel attention and admiration from a wide audience.[7] What Mansfield said in her art and how she said it are the main questions to be investigated. Whether Mansfield loses herself in her stories is the point—and whether she is inconsistent or hides the truth. No artist tried harder to give her work an honesty and forthrightness than Mansfield, approaching it with rare humility and organized dedication. Near the end of her life, she told her friend, A. R. Orage, that "there is not one [story] . . . I dare show to God."[8] Indeed, Orage reports that she entered the Gurdjieff Institute shortly before her death as much to perfect her mind, character, and personality in an attempt to alter and improve her fiction as to effect recovery from her physical ailments. To change one's attitude is to change one's life, Mansfield argued. "An artist communicates not his vision of the world, but the attitude that results in his vision, not his dream, but his dream-state." Therefore, she concludes, "a new attitude to life on the part of writers would first see life different and then make it different."[9] Though Mansfield died before she could adopt the new attitude that she hoped would lead to an improvement and a new direction for her art, the fact that she was seeking a change even though the literary world was acclaiming her current fiction is indicative of her commitment.

Mansfield wrote her stories under a variety of circumstances. There is the unformed, harsh, biting Mansfield of the *German Pension* stories,[10] obviously young and hurt and unsympathetic. There is the anguished maturity of Mansfield in "The Man without a Temperament" and "Je ne parle pas français." And there is the transcendent Mansfield of "The Daughters of the Late Colonel" and "Miss Brill" and "The Fly."

This study attempts no exhaustive treatment—or survey, even—of all Mansfield's eighty-eight stories and fragments. It seeks to isolate what is lasting and meaningful in Mansfield's contribution to literature, to examine closely both the form and the content of several of these meaningful additions to English fiction, and, at times, to show the genesis of the fiction in the pattern of the author's life experience. It does not pretend to be a critical-biographical study (so well done by Sylvia Berkman in *Katherine Mansfield: A Critical Study*); or a survey that comments on almost all the individual stories (like Saralyn R. Daly's *Katherine Mansfield*).[11] Rather, concentrating closely on the most distinguished of Katherine Mansfield's works, this study hopes to justify her right to a conspicuous place in contemporary letters.

2

The Artist as Critic

As a critic, Katherine Mansfield possesses in great measure what many of her contemporaries and successors lack: a warm, human approach to books and authors, a vivid critical personality, and a practical directness of motive and language. One may search in vain through the hundreds of pages of her collected reviews in *Novels & Novelists*,[1] or through the random remarks on writing and writers in her letters, *Journal*, and *Scrapbook* without encountering mention of symbolism, naturalism, decadence, aesthetics, point of view, and similar terms of early twentieth-century criticism that often tend to obscure the treatment of the work of art itself.

Probably because Mansfield is herself a writer, she sticks tenaciously to the contents of the book under review, implicitly posing such questions as: where does the book succeed or fail; why does it succeed or fail; if it fails, how might the failure have been avoided. Her method is extremely straightforward. Normally the criticism begins with a general statement of a problem in modern fiction: the tendency to rely on details rather than on an overall plan; the employment of undigested theories of psychoanalysis by the novelist; or the attempt to entertain and amuse in the "pastime" novel, without regard for the serious reader or for art. Such generalization is normally followed by Mansfield's recapitulation of the plot of the novel, often rendered with amused or exasperated irony so that merely giving the synopsis renders the judgment. The critical piece usually ends with the critic's return to the original generalization, but now with particular practical reference to the work under discussion.

As in her letters, Mansfield reveals a strong and sharp personality in every line of her criticism. There is no temporizing with inferior work, no praising of friends because they are friends, no puffing of a private coterie or attacks on the favorites of hostile critics. Though most of Mansfield's criticism comes from the pages of her husband's *Athenaeum*, the reviews speak with her voice and offer her judgments, not the collective judgments of the periodical. Indeed, the reviews might easily have been paragraphs in letters mailed to the authors of the works she criticizes, or to their publishers and readers. Mansfield is obviously no more self-conscious in her public examination of literature than in her private comments on books in her letters. Thus, it is perfectly possible for her to like one book by Virginia Woolf and dislike the next without worrying about her own consistency or her friend's reaction. Or to find late publication of an early work by Conrad a mistake, after he had achieved fame for much more worthwhile efforts in maturity. Or to praise an attempt at fantasy by one writer while dealing harshly with the attempt by another. To the extent that all considerations except the text under discussion can be made extraneous, Mansfield endeavors to make them so and to ignore them.

Mansfield found little to praise in most of the books she reviewed. To her lot fell the potboilers, the two-novels-a-year writers, most of whom have in half a century dropped from critical view. The names of these novelists mean nothing today even to scholars of the period—Ernest Oldmeadow, Harold Brighouse, Ashford

Owen, D. A. Barker, Patience Worth, Rhoda Broughton, and George Birmingham are typical of her critical subjects. When she did have the opportunity, occasionally, to review the work of writers of the first rank, Virginia Woolf, John Galsworthy, George Moore, E. M. Forster, Joseph Conrad, her tone is more respectful though her judgments are just as definite and, if she feels the work merits it, just as damning. It is interesting to compare her private enthusiasms in literature with the quite different fare she had to digest for review purposes. In her letters and private papers, Chekhov is the hero, almost the literary god. Joyce is frequently mentioned both with enthusiasm and with distaste. Lawrence, Flaubert, Maupassant share attention with Bunin, Proust, and T. S. Eliot. In the published prose, the work of Mary Agnes Hamilton must be approached hopefully for the kind of literary experience these others afford. How Mansfield avoids sourness on a steady diet of incompetents is the marvel.

Mansfield's criticism relates to the present study in two ways: as a gloss on the artist's own fiction and on her view of her art; and, to a lesser degree, as a source of information on Mansfield's private view of her world, as it impinges on what she and other artists write. Though this chapter will concern itself primarily with the former, at least one example of the latter should be mentioned first.

Katherine Mansfield had deep convictions about the effects of the war on humankind. She had seen intimately the reality of the war during her enforced stay in France while the bombs fell. Perhaps the most traumatic shock to her whole being had been the death of her brother Leslie just after his arrival in France as a soldier. Though John Middleton Murry had not been in active combat, she knew what years in London under war conditions had done to his health and his personality.[2] For some, the war was a patriotic escapade wherein brave men proved themselves capable of enduring inordinate pain bravely, as good Englishmen should, and of inflicting inordinate pain on the other side, while devoted wives joined auxiliary services or waited at home for the heroes to return. This simplistic and, to her, utterly false view disseminated by the popular press and by the "pastime" novels of the period, Mansfield could not abide. Those writers who presented it were treated with disdain by the critic. Writing of F. E. Penny's *Desire and Delight* in a review published just months after the armistice, Mansfield recalls the heroine's "charm":

> She is the best type of young English womanhood; it is, indeed, she, and women like her, who have made the British Empire what it is. . . . once they have secured their Eden-hope, [they] will send him off to the wars without a murmur, hear of his being wounded with a thrill of pride, and confide in their best friend that "even if Maurice died I suppose I should just have to carry on." They might, also, nurse in hospitals for months on end, and mark the terrible things that happen to a man's mind as well as his body, and still be capable of acting towards another as this newly-wedded wife acted. Why not? Surely love is stronger than war-shock? Surely, faced by a fine blooming young woman, a man should be able to forget everything else! [3]

For Gilbert Frankau's *Peter Jackson* she has only scorn for its seeking to glorify "war—dreadful, bloody, glorious, stinking frightful, magnificent war. . . . The middle of his novel is, if one examines it, nothing but a roaring hymn in praise of killing, for killing is the Job of Jobs."[4]

She is satisfied only by Vincente Blasco Ibanez's treatment of war in *The Four Horsemen*, for this foreigner sees war without the sentimental and patriotic cant of the usual English fictional treatment. Readers have become so accustomed to the depiction of war's bloody horror that they are indifferent to it, she reasons. But

Ibanez's treatment of war focuses on an old man who must stand by, watching the Germans, "staring stupidly while they break up and plunder his toy [a gold bath], and kill the innocent villagers." [5] What satisfies Mansfield's sense of the rightness of the novel most is that the author draws no inspirational message from the carnage: war to Ibanez is Hell; no good comes of it, temporal or spiritual; nor "can there be any line drawn so that here we are at war and here we are not at war." [6]

This last observation is particularly significant to Mansfield, for it supports a view that had been central to her for a long time. Writing to Murry on November 10, 1919, about a novel by Virginia Woolf that she is currently reviewing for the *Athenaeum* (*Night and Day*, reviewed on November 14, 1919), Mansfield admits that "I don't like it. . . . My private opinion is that it is a lie in the soul. The war never has been: that is what its message is. . . . the novel can't just leave the war out. There *must* have been a change of heart. It is really fearful to see the 'settling down' of human beings." She goes on to declare that "nothing can ever be the same—that, as artists, we are traitors if we feel otherwise." Therefore, she concludes, the war must be considered and artists must "find new expressions, new moulds for our new thoughts and feelings." [7] Her example is apt. Jane Austen could not, in the twentieth-century environment, write *Northanger Abbey*. A year later (September 25, 1920) she is still expressing incredulity that "writers who have lived through our times can *drop* these last ten years and revert to why Edward didn't understand Vi's reluctance to be seduced or (see Bennett) why a dinner of twelve covers needs remodelling." What disturbs her most is the utter lack of "continuity" in writers like these whose works appear forged in a vacuum, without regard to the real world of yesterday or today.[8]

The student of Mansfield's criticism may begin with

her aversion to the standard novel about the war in terms of her own personal, autobiographical reaction to the holocaust. Before long, however, as the paragraphs just written testify, he finds it impossible to separate her private emotional response from her response as an alert intellectual, as a perceptive critic. This is as it should be according to Mansfield, for the primary requirement of the artist is not facility with language, or knowledge of his characters, or even emotional sensitivity. What the artist needs above all else is to take "a *long look* at life. He says softly, 'So this is what life is, is it?' And he proceeds to express that. All the rest he leaves." [9]

In specific terms, the problem of the artist in expressing "life" is to relate his fictional characters to this broader spectrum, this continuity, the universe, history, in short, to whatever appropriate universal applies. And Mansfield's lament in most instances is that the English novelists she reviews are not up to this task, for their "*long look*" falls short of the mark. European novelists, she finds, have less trouble establishing the required relationship. Reviewing Louis Couperus's *Old People and the Things that Pass* (December 12, 1919), she sums up foreign superiority in this way:

> What is it then that differentiates these living characters from the book-bound creatures of even our brilliant modern English writers? Is it not that the former are seen ever, and always in relation to life—not to a part of life, not to a set of society, but to the bounding horizon, life, and the latter are seen in relation to an intellectual idea of life? In this second case life is made to fit them. . . . But life cannot be made to "fit" anybody, and the novelist who makes the attempt will find himself cutting something that gets smaller and smaller . . . until he must begin cutting his characters next to fit the thing he has made.[10]

Dorothy Richardson's *Interim* is criticized, along with lesser novels, for this fault. The experiences in the book may be well described but they remain isolated experiences, unrelated to the rest of life. Richardson and the others are "content to remain in the air, hovering over, as if the thrilling moment were enough and more than enough." Richardson's presentation of these experiences of Miriam Henderson in novel after novel, "leaves us feeling, as before, that everything being of equal importance . . . it is impossible that everything should not be of equal unimportance." What interests the reader about people, or about characters in a book is "to see them in their relation to Life as we know it," not to view them in discrete isolation like portraits on a wall.[11] Failure to supply these indispensable relationships in fiction is responsible for the pettiness of postwar English fiction.

Furthermore, Mansfield ascribes the failure in her eyes of the then-popular psychological study, the slice-of-life case history in fiction, to the same inability to relate characters to the larger fabric of the world. Criticizing May Sinclair's *Mary Olivier: A Life,* Mansfield notes the deliberate attempt of the author and her school to "represent things and persons as separate, as distinct, as apart as possible." In her analogy, the critic sees the characters as animals, one species different from the other in certain obvious ways, and each one studied minutely. But "where is the Ark? And where, even at the back of the mind, is the Flood. . . . The Ark and the Flood belong to the old order, they are gone." Authors like Sinclair now simply ask, "What is the effect of this animal upon me, or this or the other one?" [12]

In her jeremiads against such discontinuity, such fragmentation, such loss of universal framework and mythical base, Mansfield reveals herself as one more heir to the discoveries of physics and psychology, and an unwilling heir at that. Writing in a transitional period, she antedates T. E. Eliot's approval of Joyce's technique for rendering the impossible contemporary world in his "Ulysses: Order and Myth"; and she anticipates Virginia Woolf's diatribe against the deadness of literature by accretion in "Mr. Bennett and Mrs. Brown," which was not to appear until several years later. Like Woolf, who explained that "life is not a series of gig-lamps symmetrically arranged," but rather "a luminous halo" in which human beings interacted in accordance with a pattern that was larger than they, Mansfield believed that the author's role was to demonstrate such a pattern. It is especially interesting, therefore, that she was unable to appreciate the elaborate patternings attempted by Joyce in *Ulysses* or Proust in his epic of time.

Katherine Mansfield's insistence that characters be related to their world is matched by her critical demand that they be living, credible people in their own right, not merely pawns on a patterned board. "What it *boils down to* is . . . [ellipsis Mansfield's] 'either the man can make his people live and keep 'em alive or he can't,'" Mansfield tells Middleton Murry on September 25, 1920.[13] One way to "keep 'em alive" Mansfield describes in a later note to her husband (November 3, 1920): it is to identify with one's creations. Explaining that she has just completed a story of New Zealand called "The Stranger," she excitedly proclaims:

> I've *been* this man, *been* this woman. I've stood for hours on the Auckland Wharf. I've been out in the stream waiting to be berthed—I've been a seagull hovering at the stern and a hotel porter whistling through his teeth. It isn't as though one sits and watches the spectacle. That would be thrilling enough, God knows. But one IS the spectacle for the time.[14]

Mansfield recognizes that few writers have attained such a degree of involvement, but her criticism constantly takes to task the great and the small who fail to give their characters a life of their own. Edith Wharton in

The Age of Innocence produces "portraits," human beings "arranged for exhibition purposes, framed, glazed, and hung in the perfect light." [15] Galsworthy's Soames Forsyte of *In Chancery* is unhappily "an appearance only—a lifelike image," and this flaw helps to render the book less artistically valuable than *The Man of Property*.[16] Maugham's Charles Strickland, in *The Moon and Sixpence*, fails to convince because his motivations are never given.[17]

The plot to Mansfield is subordinate to the depiction of character. More than once she judges the novels of Sheila Kaye-Smith failures because her characters are employed merely as mouthpieces for advancing the plot, and therefore "it does not seem to matter whether they speak, feel or think. Nothing is gained by it. They are just what they are. The plot's the thing." [18]

If the "feeling for life" is put ahead of the "feeling for writing," then Mansfield believes that, as with Jane Austen's work, the novel will have a powerful effect on the reader and the characters will live long after the book is put down. But when these antithetical feelings alternate uneasily, as in Virginia Woolf's *Night and Day*, many of the characters become lifeless as the reader lays the novel aside. "We have the queer sensation that once the author's pen is removed from them they have neither speech nor motion, and are not to be revived again until she adds another stroke or two or writes another sentence underneath." [19] Mrs. Humphry Ward comes in for even harsher treatment as a sheltered, intellectual, theoretical social worker of literature, ushering her puppetlike characters into the library for decorous delivery of messages about life's problems and then sending them out to oblivion. "She had no idea of what happened to those people when they had left the library" and no concern "beyond a kind of professional sympathetic interest." [20] There is no doubt in Mansfield's mind, apparently, that neither writer had, like herself, "*been*" the people they portrayed.

To take Mansfield's extravagant pronouncements on the undesirability of intellectual primacy in art as evidence of a loose attitude toward the discipline of composition is to be falsely put off by the critic's enthusiasm for vivid characterization. No critic who is also a practicing artist is more rigorous in his demand that the writer be in firm control of his material and his pen. In one letter, Mansfield insists that every word of a story must be in place and that no word be capable of deletion if the fiction is ideally fashioned. To Dorothy Brett, her painter friend, she confesses her belief in technique "because I don't see how art is going to make that divine *spring* into the bounding outline of things if it hasn't passed through the process of trying to become these things before re-creating them." [21]

That is why she rejects "note-book literature" (Samuel Butler had advised young writers to keep notebooks, but Mansfield complains that in her time writers offer their notebooks as the finished work of art) as sloppy and second-rate. Virginia Woolf's *Kew Gardens* is praised precisely because it is *not* random and haphazard, but firm, contrived, inevitable.[22] Virginia Sackville-West's *Heritage* is criticized because, essentially, the author loses "control" and allows her effective style to be abused by lack of meaningful manipulation of narrators.[23] May Sinclair's *Mary Olivier* is a profusion of undifferentiated surface impressions in which reader and writer have lost the thread of the "mystery of life."[24] What satisfies in a work of art is the feeling that the artist "was master of the situation when he wrote it" so the sense of shape and meaningfulness is essential. Notebooks and lists of facts cannot be substituted for this artistic contrivance.

Intellectual and artistic control means too the deliberate imposition of restrictions on excessive and extraneous verbiage. For Mansfield, Joseph Hergesheimer's *Linda Condon* would have been a much more successful novel had the author resisted the temptation to register "every pink-silk box of black chocolates, every cocktail, bath extract, perfume, sugared fig, quilted bed cover, web of lingerie." Not to do so is to "smother" the author's central idea. It means also, as Sheila Kaye-Smith had not learned in *Green Apple Harvest*, a deliberate decision with respect to the tone that a piece of fiction should display: it cannot presume to be a country novel, with dialect and pastoral lack of sophistication, on the one hand, and, on the other, a poeticized prose piece of rarefied urban flavor.[25] In these respects, Mansfield's mature short stories are the best examples of an authorial balance between conscious cerebration and, for want of a better term, what may be termed inspired imaginative manipulation.

But control to what end? Mansfield supplies both an emotional and an intellectual answer. In a letter to Murry (November 21, 1920), she replies to his praise of her "Miss Brill" by saying that she "liked her, too. One writes (*one* reason why is) because one does care so passionately that one *must show* it—one must declare one's love."[26] But in her *Scrapbook* a year later, and under the influence of Hegel, she reasons that the artist's motive for creation is to construct his own world within the world as he finds it. This, she points out, is quite different from the writer attempting to "impose his vision of life upon the existing world." Like Joyce, she insists that the artist must not "grind an axe." This way of looking at the role of the artist precludes the possibility that reality may become the ideal. "That which suggests the subject to the artist is the *unlikeness* to what we accept as reality. We [the artists] single out—we bring into the light—we put up higher."[27] Such a view seems close to

Joyce's in his explanation of the function of his epiphanies.

To bring into the light, to put up higher, Mansfield recognized, called for departures from traditional fiction both in content and form, and in review after review she was quick to announce the need for experiment. For the "safe" novelist, who leads his public only into places which he knows they will be comfortable in, she feels contempt, and she advises F. Brett Young, for one, to "forget the impatient public" and go in fiction where his material carries him without regard to audience approval.[28] She reproves Galsworthy with good-humored patience for his attack on the "new school" of writers, expressing at the same time her disbelief that there was indeed a "school" worthy of the designation.[29]

When Katherine Mansfield called for the "experimental' 'in art, she was wise enough to distinguish between novelty and the significantly new. The amateur writer, she could see, "begins as an experimentalist; the true artist ends as one," by carrying his fiction into uncharted territory. Joseph Conrad's career exemplifies for her the role of this true artist as experimentalist, for he has refused to repeat himself, after his initial success with the public, and his latest book is always "new." [30]

More interesting than Mansfield's pronouncements in the abstract on the current "age of experiment" is her reaction to particular experiments in fiction that came to her notice. In this regard, it may be said with fairness that her sincerity and enthusiasm as a harbinger of newness were often accompanied by an uneasiness and a bewilderment with what the postwar literary harvest had brought forth. Reviewing *Three Lives,* Mansfield is obviously disturbed by what she considers the frivolousness of Gertrude Stein's method.

> Miss Gerturde Stein has discovered a new way of writing stories. It is just to keep right on writing them. Don't mind

how often you go back to the beginning, don't hesitate to say the same thing over and over again—people are always repeating themselves—don't be put off if the words sound funny at times: just keep right on, and by the time you've done writing you'll have produced your effect.

She complains that after a while, she found herself unconsciously reading Stein in "*syncopated time*," and the review ends with an invocation to heaven to prevent Gertrude Stein from becoming a fashion.[31] Clearly, Mansfield not only does not sympathize with Stein's attempt at experimentation in prose; she does not even understand the terms of the experiment. Though the reviewer is impelled to render the effect of the book upon her in musical terms—rhythm, repetition, ragtime, Southern orchestra, banjos, the silent singing of the reader taken unawares—it never occurs to Mansfield to view the work seriously in musical terms, as an attempt artistically to blend the two arts. Or to set up for a work that, on its surface, needs special rules, a critical framework against which it may be placed for judgment. Stein is merely laughed off.

In not quite so cavalier a fashion, Mansfield's uneasiness is exhibited when she reads Joyce's *Ulysses*. Having acknowledged that Joyce is "immensely important,"[32] she admits her inability to "get over a great great deal." "I can't get over the feeling of wet linoleum and unemptied pails and far worse horrors in the house of his mind—He's so terribly *unfein*. . . . One can stand much, but that kind of shock which is the result of vulgarity and commonness, one is frightened of receiving."[33] By May of 1922, the shock of January had abated and the judgment, in a letter to Dorothy Brett (May 1) is considerably sounder. Conceding the difficulty and obscurity, Mansfield now found that Joyce's intention was not at all to shock by coarseness. And though she still doesn't "*approve* of what he's done," she admires the characterization of Bloom and "Marian."[34] Three months later she tells Violet Schiff (August 24) that Joyce's masterpiece is fading from her memory. "As to reading it again, or even opening that great tome—never!" The publication of a book like *Ulysses* was "inevitable," she concludes and its appearance ought be considered a "portentous warning" of the way literature is moving.[35]

Except for Mansfield's praise of Joyce's characterization, there is little indication of an orientation toward the modern spirit in Mansfield's strictures, much less indeed than in the views of lesser writers on the new novel. For her to be, as she declares herself in her *Scrapbook* in 1922, "dead *against* it" is a rather uncritical position. "I suppose it was worth doing if everything is worth doing . . . [ellipsis Mansfield's] but that is certainly not what I want from literature."[36]

Nor did she want the spate of psychoanalytical novels that appeared after the war. On October 13, 1920, she writes Murry of her amazement at the growth of "cheap psychoanalysis" in the fiction that she reads:

And I want to prove it won't do—it's turning Life into a *case*. And yet, of course, I do believe one ought to be able to—not ought—one's novel if it's a good one will be capable of being *proved* scientifically to be correct. Here—the thing that's happening now is—*the impulse to write is a different impulse*. With an artist—one has to allow—Oh tremendously—for the subconscious element in his work. He writes he knows not what—he's *possessed*. . . . Now these people who are nuts on analysis seem to me to have *no* subconscious at all. They write to *prove*—not to tell the truth.[37]

Mansfield's complaint is not then with Freud or Jung nor with psychoanalysis as a scientific method of treatment, but rather with literary opportunists who falsify and cheapen not only the science itself but the fictional mould into which it is poured. In a review of a psychoanalytical novel, she complains that the book is a work of explanation, not of creation, for in the very act of explaining, the author first fails to be concerned with the development of his characters *as* characters in a story; then fails to pay proper attention to the language in which he writes, preferring the bluntest, most "scientific" approach; and finally, even if the situation in the novel and its development is perfectly clear, the psychoanalytical novelist feels impelled to provide a lengthy and superfluous technical "explanation." Even May Sinclair, for whose devotion and reputation Mansfield has respect, has declined as a writer as she has adopted the method of the psychoanalysts.

Some degree of personal involvement must be allowed for here in Mansfield's evaluation. The heart of her short fiction had always been psychological portraiture—the revelation of life through the subtle revelation of character. Yet in all Mansfield's mature stories, there is no "explanation." There is no scientific jargon. There is certainly no attempt to reproduce the aura of the sick-room. If the two daughters of the late colonel owe their quavering, wavering old-maidishness to an unwholesome relationship with their father (their mother died young), Mansfield will convey the possibility through subtleties of association (attraction for moon, affinity toward sun, the buddha figure, and so forth), never through direct explanation of the relationship, scientific or not. To stint on this richness of possibility, to reduce human beings to cases all of whose symptoms are capable of treatment medically, struck not only at her sense of literary fitness but personally at the method she had painfully evolved for telling the truth in fiction. Yet, aside from this biographical fact, there is no doubt that Mansfield was correct in her diagnosis of the weakness of these early attempts at literary psychoanalysis.

It is probably fair to say that, on the whole, Mansfield

neither insisted upon modernity as a requirement of postwar writing nor rejected it summarily. Like all sound critics, she examined each work individually and did her best to cope with the problems it presented—problems of expression, interpretation, point of view, tone, and the like. She might reject *Ulysses* as not being to her taste, but almost in the same breath she writes to Violet Schiff that Eliot's *Prufrock* is "by far and away the most interesting and the best modern poem." [38] At the same time, she could be thrilled by the verse of Walter de la Mare. She accepts the modernity of D. H. Lawrence [39] with enthusiasm while failing to appreciate Gertrude Stein. She calls for new ways in fiction to express the new world though simultaneously she welcomes Virginia Woolf's *Night and Day* specifically *because* it smacks of the conventional novel: "We had thought that this world was vanished for ever, that it was impossible to find on the great ocean of literature a ship that was unaware of what has been happening. Yet here is 'Night and Day' fresh, new and exquisite, a novel in the tradition of the English novel. . . . We had never thought to look upon its like again!" [40]

Certainly Mansfield was more at home with the traditionalists than with the avant garde. Her personal preference—almost adoration—for Chekhov is one of the constants of an otherwise disorderly life. Not content with reading his work in English, she translated his stories from the Russian, adapted (some say plagiarized) more than one of them, collaborated with S. S. Koteliansky on a translation of Chekhov's letters and papers, and generally acted as his most enthusiastic disciple in England.[41] Again, some of the affinity is literary, some strictly personal. Chekhov sought to accomplish in the Russian short story what Mansfield tried to do in the English. Both leave to revelation of character the principal share of the story, the author and his "explanation" remaining well out of it. Both subordinate plot to psychological probing to the extent that they have had to share the guilt of formlessness and ostensible lack of direction in their narrative. Both are concerned with the middle class as it provides ammunition for social satire; yet for both the satire is subordinate to the presentation of character.

But Mansfield found much more than a literary predecessor in Chekhov; she found in him a surrogate for herself—and she knew it. In her *Journal,* she asks him why he is dead and unable to converse with her. She often invokes him as though calling on her own inner resources—or on God.[42] And in a deeply revealing letter to Murry (October 15, 1922), just a few weeks before her death, she demonstrates her knowledge of their similarity of situation.

> About being like Tchekhov. . . . Don't forget he died at 43. That he spent—how much? of his life chasing about in a desperate search after health. . . . Read the last [letter of Chekhov!] All hope is over for him. Letters are deceptive at any rate. It's true he had occasional happy moments. But for the last 8 years he knew no *security* at all. We know he felt his stories were not half what they might be. It doesn't take much imagination to picture him on his deathbed thinking "I have never had a real chance. Something has been all wrong."[43]

Nor can Mansfield's devotion to Chekhov be ascribed merely to infatuation with Russian literature, for as critic she was just as likely to find fault with Russian fiction as to praise it. Writing to Lady Ottoline Morrell on November 13, 1918, she finds Maxim Gorki "wonderfully sympathetic" in his *Journal of the Revolution.* Some three years later, she confides to William Gerhardi (June 14, 1922) that, except for "The Gentleman from San Francisco," she doesn't "care much" for Bunin's short stories. Her evaluation of Bunin, she says, is based on his trying "too hard," his insistence on pressing his point until it is too obvious. In the same paragraph, however, she confesses to having been personally disappointed in her meeting with Bunin when he shrugged off her mention of Chekhov with a casual and hurried, "Il a écrit des belles choses." [44]

Mansfield was probably less influential as a critic than as a practitioner of fiction. In the less than two short years that she contributed to the *Athenaeum*,[45] she was hardly in a position to impose a commanding critical presence upon the literary community—even if her health and the books which she was given for review allowed. To select individuals who admired her own artistry, her opinion had the force of law. But this critical influence was normally exercised in private letters to the writer, to William Gerhardi, for instance, who had asked for comment on his work. To the public at large, she undoubtedly remained the romantic, exiled artist, and her short, acerb notices of current books occasioned more interest in the figure who wrote them than in the commentary itself.

That this should have been so is not surprising in view of the body of Mansfield's criticism itself. Unlike Eliot, or Kenneth Burke, or I. A. Richards, she offered nothing new or startling—no "objective correlative" or behavioristic rules for judging a work or special vocabulary. She insisted merely on the old critical standbys whether for evaluating new works or old. With Chekhov and Flaubert, she stressed the need for irony and distance and traced, for instance, the increasing weakness of Galsworthy as novelist to his diminishing employment of both from *The Man of Property* to *In Chancery*, particularly in his development of the character of Soames Forsyte.[46] Her attack on Jack London, in similar vein, is for his sentimentality in dealing with characters that are human, though she finds his treatment of animals quite satisfactory.[47] Sincerity in fiction is to her a major virtue, though sincerity without control won't do the trick. Like any well-balanced reader-critic, she is against superficiality (this is Joseph Hergesheimer's fault),[48] and for gaiety in the English novel to offset the dreadful seriousness of postwar fiction. Such practical, level-headed literary opinions may be very helpful to young writers and to readers who want guidance in buying the new novels, but they are not calculated to encourage bohemian coteries. If Mansfield had not written remarkable short stories, she would not be remembered today for her criticism.

3

"Prelude" and "At the Bay"

Though the death of her younger brother at the front had left her emotionally and spiritually shaken, it appears to have strengthened Katherine Mansfield's literary intentions. She would turn her mind and her pen toward her New Zealand childhood, she affirms in her first *Journal* entry for 1916, not only as a means of keeping close to her brother in memory but to pay a "debt of love" to her people there and to the land itself.[1] There was much material at hand, for, unlike most young apprentices, Mansfield had not dealt extensively hitherto with the country of her birth. Privately a little contemptuous of it (after tasting academic and bohemian life in London), she had dealt occasionally with her childhood but never as a celebration of the country as a country. In fact, her first book is devoted to a delineation of Germany if one takes it in the broadest sense possible. Now she would double back on her tracks to make a new and more significant start. Her recent successes in the short story now appeared petty. The characters she had created seemed to have no place in the new vision of life and art that had come to her. The plots seemed forced and unnatural.

Recognition of the utter unsatisfactoriness of her past efforts and understanding of the ambitiousness of the new enterprise brought Mansfield's work to a halt for several weeks. One does not undertake lightly the recreation of a world and the reawakening of its inhabitants.

Oh, I want for one moment to make our undiscovered country leap into the eyes of the Old World. It must be mysterious, as though floating. It must take the breath. . . . all must be told with a sense of mystery, a radiance, an afterglow.[2]

In short, the place described must come alive as it was, but the writer must overlay the ordinary with Wordsworth's cloak of the imagination.

When finally the words did come, the results were "Prelude" and "At the Bay," the most extensive and elaborate of Mansfield's efforts in fiction. Precisely what these short stories say has eluded critics since their publication. One writer sees in them a marvel of description of nature. Another praises them for illuminating the world of childhood. Another sees in their ostensible episodic patternlessness a recreation of the haphazardness of life. To still another, the stress is on the willing alienation of the sensitive individual in an unfriendly world. There is almost no detailed examination of these important literary documents, however, in the half century since their publication.[3]

One way to approach these stories is through a remark of Mansfield to Dorothy Brett in a letter dated March 9, 1922. In it, she denies that "all beauty is marred by ugliness."

I don't feel quite that. For it seems to me if Beauty were Absolute it would no longer be the kind of Beauty it is. Beauty triumphs over ugliness in Life. That's what I feel. And that marvelous triumph is what I long to express.

"Life," she concludes in the same letter, "is, all at one and the same time, far more mysterious and far simpler than we know. It's like religion in that."[4] Four years earlier, she had revealed her "secret belief" to Lady Ottoline Morrell that, though life was full of ugliness and baseness, "there is something at the back of it all—which if only I were great enough to understand would make *everything*, everything, indescribably beautiful.[5] "Prelude" and "At the Bay" seem Mansfield's attempt to demonstrate in art the triumph of beauty over ugliness, mystery over simplicity, artistic "knowledge" over natural baseness.

The form of "Prelude" is episodic, "more or less my own invention," Mansfield told Dorothy Brett on October 11, 1917.[6] There is no doubt that Mansfield intended it to be so. The "Notes for 'Prelude' " in the *Scrapbook* for 1916 divide the story into apparently disconnected bits and pieces: "Stanley Burnell drives home; the Nursery; Beryl with a guitar; Children; Alice. . . ." [7] There is further evidence in her letter to Dorothy Brett that the episodic form was chosen to approximate in prose the meteorological conditions of New Zealand "just as on those mornings [of Mansfield's New Zealand youth] white milky mists rise and uncover some beauty, then smother it again and then again disclose it, I tried to lift that mist from my people and let them be seen and then to hide them again." [8]

The twelve episodes combine to tell a simple story. In the first, the children prepare to leave their old home for a new house further out in the suburbs. In the second, Kezia, the surrogate for Katherine Mansfield, surveys for the last time the empty rooms of the house. Part three describes the drive of the children and the coachman to the new house, where they are put to bed by the grandmother while the other adult members of the family help with the unpacking. The fourth part describes how the members of the family go off to sleep: Aunt Beryl dreaming of the love she does not yet possess, Kezia afraid of the dark, Linda and Stanley, Kezia's parents, in a matrimonial scene, and so forth. The next episode describes the parents rising in the morning; the sixth takes up relationships among the grandmother and her two daughters, Beryl and Linda; the seventh deals with Stanley's return from the office to his home; the eighth, the children at play; the ninth, the reaction of the children to the killing of a duck by the handyman; the tenth, the activities of the housemaid and her relationship to Beryl; the eleventh, Linda's thoughts on life, love, childbearing, and other intimate subjects; and the last episode deals with Beryl's introspection and self-analysis.

Yet, having said this about the story, the critic has said nothing, for the significance of "Prelude" resides, as Mansfield well knew, in its sometimes subtle, sometimes blatant patterns of association: its repetitions of images and symbols in diverse contexts, its choice of metaphors, its arrangement of the order of narration, and its almost musically evocative rendering of existence.

Mansfield's choice of title illustrates her meaningful employment of association. "Prelude" is as broad a title and a term as might have been chosen. Prelude to what? is the question. For the family, the move from one house to another is prelude to a new kind of suburban living. For the children, especially Kezia, the period described and the experiences encountered are a prelude to growing into adolescence. For Beryl, the move may be the first step to spinsterhood, involving as it does her isolation from eligible young men. Old age, for the grandmother, can be, and is shown to be in "At the Bay," a prelude to death. For Linda and Stanley, it appears to represent no special alteration of the marital relationship.

Throughout the story, however, Mansfield intrudes the image of "swelling" and its attendant associations. First Kezia tells the storeman that she often dreams "that animals rush at me—even camels—and while they are rushing, their heads swell e-enormous [*sic*]" (p. 225).[9] Shortly thereafter, the author describes a similar dream of Kezia's mother, Linda, who, as she strokes a small bird, finds that it too starts to "swell." "It grew bigger and bigger. . . . It had become a baby with a big naked head and a gaping bird-mouth" (p. 231). In an apparently unrelated episode, the reader learns that, as a baby, Beryl had been stung by an ant "and how the child's leg had swelled. . . . how terrifying it was" (p. 235).

Mansfield reserves to the aloe planted on a strip of lawn in front of the new house the most revealing mention of swelling:

> Linda looked up at the fat swelling plant with its cruel leaves and fleshy stem. High above them, as though becalmed in the air, and yet holding so fast to the earth it grew from, it might have had claws instead of roots. The curving leaves seemed to be hiding something; the blind stem cut into the air as if no wind could ever shake it.
>
> "That is an aloe, Kezia," said her mother.
>
> "Does it ever have any flowers?"
>
> "Yes, Kezia," and Linda smiled down at her, and half shut her eyes. "Once every hundred years." (p. 240)

This aloe plant, which gives its name to the first version of "Prelude," is the principal symbol of the story and lends perspective to the title and the "swelling" image. For this great rooted blossomer is in certain respects like Linda and in certain others ironically very different. Though "fat" and "swelling" and capable of bearing fruit, it must endure the process once each century. Linda's problem, on the other hand, is a daily fear of the brutality of sex even with a husband she loves, and an indifference to motherhood as a calling. "I shall go on having children," she muses wryly, "and the children and the gardens will grow bigger and bigger with whole fleets of aloes in them for me to choose from" (p. 258).

In her eyes, when she contemplates Stanley's sexual role, he becomes "my Newfoundland dog" (p. 257) who rushes at her and frightens her. In this sense, the swelling becomes as much sexual as maternal, and her admiration for the "long sharp thorns" (p. 257) of the aloe as protection against violation is a lament for the shield she herself lacks. No wonder, then, that the aloe's infrequency of bearing induces her to adopt that plant as her means of escape, at least in fantasy, and she sees herself riding the aloe as a ship, the grassy bank having become in her dream-state the waves of a body of water (p. 257).

Swelling has now been associated with the sexual act, with pregnancy, and with the blossoming and fruition that these imply. It is easier to see now the relevance of the random conversation at the beginning of section eight between Mrs. Jones and Mrs. Smith (Everywoman to Anywoman?) regarding children: "I brought both my twins. I have another baby since I saw you last, but she came so suddenly that I haven't had time to make her any clothes, yet" (p. 246). Obviously, the average woman is not an aloe in her breeding habits. Obviously too, when Stanley sees the empty place at the top of the family table and thinks, "That's where my boy ought to sit" (p. 244), he is, in a sense, heralding the arrival of the baby Linda will have by the time of "At the Bay."

Mansfield has, then, written "Prelude" as an annunciation of the birth of her brother. Though he is not in the story as a living character, the whole narrative is but prelude to the swelling act of his coming. And, as in "The Garden Party" and other stories, the author has chosen to root the characters in the world of nature. The grandmother is Mrs. *Fairfield* in whose mothering soil Linda feels more comfortable than almost anywhere else—as the aloe holds "fast to the earth it grew from" (p. 240). Linda herself has a name that recalls the linden tree ("linda" in Old High German), and the yellow blossoms she admires and philosophizes about in "At the Bay" are characteristic of the linden tree in bloom. Even the unusual name of Kezia is from the English "cassia," identifying a genus of shrubs and trees. Perhaps the female characters are named in this fashion as one further means of universalizing this principal motif of generation of life. This is not the story merely of the birth of "the boy," Mansfield's brother, but the very intricate, though basically simple, exposition of birth, maturity, generation, and death from the beginning to the end of time. It is a natural process, and thus beautiful, but tinged with the occasional uglinesses of existence in this world.

Looked at in this way, the story assumes a more definite shape than, at first reading, it seems to have. Mrs. Fairfield is presented almost tritely, certainly conventionally, as the patterner of life. She carries out patterns in the crocheting[10] which is never far from her fingers as well as in all the other feminine domestic tasks that fall to her. She imposes the shaping force on the new kitchen so that there is not any question of who has been at work putting objects in pairs and otherwise arranging chaos into order. In all respects, she assumes the mother role that Linda seems unwilling to fulfill toward her children.

Mansfield also is concerned to establish a kinship between the two younger female figures, vaguely in terms of their presumptive candidature for motherhood. Mainly this is accomplished by assigning to Linda and Kezia, mother and daughter, almost identical dream patterns which are subsequently transferred to patterns of fear. In the second part of "Prelude," Kezia is frightened because "IT was just behind her, waiting at the door, at the head of the stairs" (p. 223). A few pages further on, she hates "rushing animals like dogs and parrots. I often dream that animals rush at me—e camels—and while they are rushing, their heads swell e-enormous" (p. 225). Similarly, Linda dreams of birds and fears "because THEY were there" (p. 234), and fears, at night, her "Newfoundland dog" (p. 257), her aggressive husband Stanley. In using almost identical imagery for mother and daughter's dreams and fears—especially in identifying the source of the fear in both instances by capitalized personal pronouns—Mansfield must have wanted to call attention to the similarities between them. But since they are not particularly alike in their personalities or characters or in their relationships with their environment, the attempt appears to be to pair them (as Grandmother Fairfield pairs objects in the kitchen) only in their roles as females who are likely to undergo the trauma of sex and pregnancy and birth. There is a suggestion too of a broad patterning into present, past, and future in the story, somewhat in the manner of Thomas Mann in his "Disorder and Early Sorrow," but the motif, if present, fails to justify itself thematically.

Like Virginia Woolf, Mansfield deals at length—if less explicitly—with the question of identity in "Prelude." The notion that human beings adopt masks and present themselves to their fellows under assumed personalities was, as has been pointed out, one of Mansfield's personal beliefs as well as one of her literary obsessions.[11] "Prelude" allows her to deal at length with the phenomenon, though she has nothing startlingly new to offer in the story. Stanley Burnell is shown first as the world sees him: stiff, demanding in his personal relationships, proper to the point of fussiness. There is flashback in time to the way he appeared to Linda before he became a suitor—quite a different view from the one he presents to her now and the one he presents to those outside the family circle. Linda ruminates on how his real self is displayed only to her, and that only in their most intimate moments: Stanley at prayer, Stanley in his male role. Even as she ruminates, however, Linda exhibits her own dual nature: she is not merely the sickly, lazy, rather colorless young mother outsiders see; she feels deeply and has insight into her own emotions. The reader who begins by being slightly contemptuous of her finds himself altering his earlier view.

The problem of identity is most directly faced by Linda's sister Beryl, both in this story and in "At the Bay." Deliberately, Beryl, whose name comes from a precious mineral whose shade hovers between green and blue and whose depths seem at times opaque, at times transparent, is permitted to examine introspectively her own dual nature. In the act of writing a letter to her friend, she is almost surprised to discover that the self she has been presenting in it is alien to her: "It was her other self who had written that letter. It not only bored, it rather disgusted her real self" (p. 260). When she looks into the mirror, the girl who looks back at her seems also a different person. And though Beryl is most unhappy to recognize that she is figuratively two-faced, she is powerless to bring the two parts of her being, the girl and the mask, together. Attributing the existence of the two aspects to her unhappiness, which necessitates adopting a false front, helps her to bear her burden but in no way eliminates it. Unlike Stanley, however, Beryl has the insight to recognize her two selves. Bumbling Stanley, like most of the men Mansfield creates in fiction, is capable of infinite self-deception and rationalizes his discrete attitudes so that they seem to form an integrated pattern of behavior.

This theme of identity—of the masks human beings put on—appears to be part of the larger motif of illusion and reality in life which permeates "Prelude." Mansfield might have been attracted to the theme through a reading of Chekhov, where it looms so large, or of Joyce, whose *Dubliners*, published shortly before Mansfield wrote "Prelude," is solidly rooted in the motif.[12] It is more likely, however, that the choice of theme was personal rather than literary. For Mansfield, the difference between what was and what might have been was enormous. The gulf between the desirable and the possible seemed impassible. Her private papers are full of her sympathy for Keats [13] as he cries out in letter after letter at the cruelty of life which dangles happiness before a person but will not allow him to reach out for it. The same impulse somehow to snatch joy from the illusion of happiness that prompted Keats to write "The Eve of St. Agnes" undoubtedly shaped Mansfield's response to the world, for she very explicitly defines Keats's problem as analogous to her own and despairs of practical solutions.

In her fiction, therefore, and particularly in "Prelude," the real self and the false self are presented side by side, the dream vies with the waking life, fulfillment comes in fantasy when it cannot come in reality, and, in general, things are not what they seem. This thematic structure is especially congenial to a story in which children play a large part. The journey by night of Lottie and Kezia to their new home allows Mansfield to delineate the fantasy world of childhood that, later, is shown to be the world of adults too, though perhaps in a more sophisticated way. The everyday world puts on a mask at night and appears entirely different to the children, just as the parrots on the wallpaper are harmless while Kezia is awake but fearsome in the dream of rushing birds. Later, when the children play in the afternoon, their whole play world is the realm of fantasy, as they go from playing "hospital" to playing "ladies," in a succession of deliberate departures from reality.

The point appears to be that the adults, in childlike

fashion, continue the practice of evading reality. Linda has the same anxiety dreams as her daughter, and, even when awake, spends most of her time in the reader's view in the world of her imagination. Indeed, the central image of the aloe derives its entire symbolic raison d'être from the way in which Linda's fantasy operates upon it. Stanley Burnell attempts, in Conrad's words, to "follow the dream," [14] to live up to the ideal image of himself that his fantasy creates. Beryl has to substitute the world of illusion for the unsatisfactory world of her new home in the country. Her adolescent craving for romance cannot be satisfied by life among the women of the family, and her sense of integrity will not let her easily attempt the seduction of her brother-in-law. The only answer is to create in fantasy an ideal lover and to imagine a relationship impossible in her present existence. Even Alice the servant girl, in her separate world of the kitchen, is shown as addicted to dream books from which she attempts to interpret the realm of the fantastic and give guidance for the real life she has to live: "Alice was a mild creature in reality, but she had the most marvellous retorts ready for questions that she knew would never be put to her" (p. 253). She resents the intrusion of the real into her world of dreams: "Oh, life. There was Miss Beryl. Alice dropped the knife and slipped the *Dream Book* under the butter dish" (p. 253). But this Alice in Wonderland is constantly being forced back into the reality she prefers to avoid.

Mansfield's principal associative images for rendering the illusory world are ostensibly birds and music, often combined into songs about birds. Though there is no need to enumerate a catalogue of their employment in the story, it is sufficient to note that the nature of both is particularly apt for the use to which the author puts them. Both birds and music are of this world of reality in the sense that notes on a sheet may be read and sound may be recorded and measured, or that a bird may alight on a branch or be examined in a laboratory. But, as numerous artists have noted, a bird knows also the world of the sky and, by extension, the radiant spirit world of illusion, while music, as Plato noted, puts the real world in touch with a higher world too and keeps man in touch with the fantastic. For Mansfield to combine the two as she does is a sign of her growing sophistication in use of symbol and image. Her employment of both in "Prelude" runs neck and neck with Joyce's use of similar materials in *Dubliners* and *A Portrait of the Artist.*

It is interesting to note that the two people in "Prelude" who seem untouched by fantasy are the grandmother and Pat, the coachman. Both are rendered as eminently practical, handy people. Both deal in elementals in a matter-of-fact way, the grandmother in giving pattern to kitchens and lives in such daily tasks as putting children to bed; and Pat in giving pattern to death in the memorable scene in which he kills the duck in the presence of the little children (p. 251). Apparently Mansfield intended to establish some relationship implicitly between these two quite different characters, if only in their centrality to life and death, not in a dream world but in the here and now. It is significant, perhaps, to note that Kezia is shaken by the idea of death in her talk with her grandmother in "At the Bay" as she is with Pat when he kills the duck (pp. 282–83). And in both incidents, it will be noted, the traumatic encounter ends with a deflection of the child's terror through a trivial diversion. That Mansfield considers both the grandmother and Pat strong characters, and that their strength lies mainly in their being rooted in the real world, is hardly in question. The ending of section eleven seems conclusive, as Linda and her mother stand in the garden and view nature each in her own way. For Linda, the sight initiates a flight of fantasy that removes her temporarily from things as they are. To Grandmother Fairfield, on the other hand, the same view suggests the desirability of converting nature's harvest not into something fanciful but into currant preserves to last through the winter (pp. 258–59). Again the old woman is associated with making and creation in this world, while Linda's unwillingness to create or to work with the harvest of offspring is all the more unnatural by contrast—as Stanley's self-conscious posturings in the coach are when viewed next to Pat's natural openness.

"Prelude" offers many additional associative patterns as well, but they are less central and obtrusive. Many of these have been treated in passing by Sylvia Berkman, Saralyn Daly, and Celeste Turner Wright. The garden itself is important in this story as in "The Garden Party" and "Bliss."[15] Once again the moon has its disturbing part to play in the life of a young woman. The dog is employed again as symbol. And finally, as in Joyce and Woolf, the mackintosh that Beryl sees herself wearing in fantasy is introduced as a symbol of potential sterility, aridity, and death.[16]

"At the Bay," Katherine Mansfield's sequel to "Prelude," was not written until 1921, about five years after the first story. In almost every respect it is a faithful attempt to follow the Burnell family through another series of episodes of daily life. The child whose birth is promised in "Prelude" has been added to the family, but otherwise little has changed on this day whose principal activity is the trip to the bay by almost all members of the family for the daily bathe.

Mansfield could not quite decide what she thought of the story from day to day. To Dorothy Brett (September 1921) she confided that she hoped it was good:

> It is as good as I can do, and all my heart and soul is in it. . . . It is so strange to bring the dead to life again. There's my Grandmother, back in her chair with her pink

knitting, there stalks my uncle over the grass; I feel as I write, "You are not dead, my darlings. All is remembered. I bow down to you. I efface myself so that you may live again through me in your richness and beauty." And one feels *possessed.* And then the place where it all happens. . . . And too, one tries to go deep—to speak to the secret self we all have—to acknowledge that.[17]

Yet, within a month, she again writes Dorothy Brett on October 15 to say that the *Mercury* is bringing out "that very long seaweedy story of mine *At the Bay.*" [18] To her more intimate *Journal* she confesses her uncertainty—"But now I'm not at all sure about that story. It seems to me it's a little 'wispy'—not what it might have been." And later, when the proofs come from the publisher, "it seemed to me flat, dull, and not a success at all. I was very much ashamed of it. I am." [19]

A careful reading of "At the Bay" does not substantiate Mansfield's fears that her story fell short of the mark. Although it lacks the complexity of imagery and association of "Prelude," as an artistic representation of what life is about, it is masterful.

Mansfield's technique in the story is even more maddeningly indifferent to the requirements of the contemporary explicator that a work of art be tightly constructed, each part of the thematic frame smoothly attaching to every other part, than even "Prelude" was. The relevance of each episode to the others is not always clear, and, in some instances probably does not reveal itself for the good reason that it is not there except in a nebulous, hazy fashion. When this ostensible lack of pointed relevance manifests itself, the chances are that the vagueness is deliberate and that the author is illustrating her own attitude toward the events that shape a life, for when Mansfield wants to establish pointed relevance, as in "Miss Brill," she has no difficulty in weaving a myriad of threads into a rigidly patterned whole.[20]

Perhaps the people and events of her New Zealand childhood are too close and meaningful to her to allow the kind of artful contrivance she permits herself in other more detached instances. Maybe she understands Miss Brill better than she can grasp the forces that animate the Burnells and their circle, so that in writing of the latter she treads more gingerly and leaves the patterns less clearly defined, mistier in the New Zealand haze.

But some patterns do emerge and can be dealt with. Chief among these, it may be suggested, is the motif of freedom, which is turned over and examined in its many facets. The theme had been briefly suggested in "Prelude" as Linda imagined the aloe a ship on the waves carrying her away from her wifely duties, from her husband's sexual demands, and from the natural order of life in this world: giving birth to children and caring for them until they are able to care for themselves. For her, this real world had seemed less real than the dream of escape to freedom, and the impossibility of sustaining the fantasy had consequently made even less bearable the mundane episodes of ordinary living. In "At the Bay," there is no mention of the aloe. The illusion of freedom that it evoked in the dim light, however, becomes central to the new story.

In this regard, the title becomes much less innocuous than it seems. For the bay, as a body of water to which the inhabitants of the neighborhood repair for recreation, refreshment, and health, is clearly a symbolic element. As water, it bears a heavy weight of historical, mythical, and psychological meaning: it is most broadly life itself—from which Stephen Dedalus in *A Portrait* and *Ulysses* withdraws in hydrophobic negation while hydrophile Bloom takes baths. The attitude of each major character in "At the Bay" to the water is equally significant. In addition, if the reader admits the association that water in "Prelude" has with freedom and escape, this possibility must be considered. Finally, the Jungian idea of water as an ever-moving feminine flow, the archetype of the fecund woman (our "mighty mother," Stephen Dedalus calls the sea), may be applicable here.

It is extremely meaningful that all of the major characters of the story visit the beach and the bay during the day described except for Linda who stays in the garden in the company of her infant son. Even old Mrs. Fairfield sits on the shore and supervises the children as they bathe. But Linda, out of the mainstream of life, resenting in "Prelude" the cribbage game in which Stanley and Beryl engage to pass the time, avoids contact with the water. Sitting in her "steamer chair" but on dry land, she muses appropriately upon the waste involved in nature's production of millions of blossoms that are dissipated and on her unwillingness to produce more children (pp. 277–78). Ironically as she rests immobile in the chair and in the landlocked garden, she dreams once more of escape by water as she recalls her father promising to escape with her "up a river in China" (p. 278). It is evident that Linda deals only in dream rivers and has not the courage nor the inclination to immerse herself in the real "destructive element." Even as she asks herself, "Was there no escape?" (p. 278), she is implicitly answering the question by not being at the bay.

This bay furnishes further symbolic commentary on the life Mansfield reveals. The story opens with the sheep being driven down toward the bay by the shepherd and his sheep dog in a scene of Wordsworthian naturalness principally memorable for the author's detailed sensuous description of wetness: the early morning dew, the white sea-mist, the sea itself, the little streams, the soaking bushes, and the wet beard of the shepherd. The picture of natural life, framed in wild wetness, reveals, however, certain inhibitions on absolute freedom. The sheep are controlled in their movements by dog and shepherd as the dog himself is inhibited by Florrie the cat.

The first human being to plunge into the water this morning is seemingly Stanley whose exaltation is not at the bracing chill or the manifestation of beauty but at being, simply, first. When he discovers that his brother-in-law, Jonathan Trout, is already in the water, he loses his taste for the swim and seeks to get rid of his unwanted companion, for Stanley fancies himself in a class by himself. For him, life is an exclusive affair, and moreover, a business to be negotiated profitably, without unnecessary human intercourse or waste of time. One's environment is there as a backdrop against which the drama of the ego is played, nor does he ever lose himself in contact with life. With Jonathan, it is quite the opposite. A "Trout" in the water, he gives himself to life easily and wholeheartedly.

> That was the way to live—carelessly, recklessly, spending oneself. . . . To take things easy, not to fight against the ebb and flow of life, but to give way to it—that was what was needed. . . . To live—to live! (p. 267)

Even Mansfield's language, it will be noted, juxtaposes "life" and "ebb and flow" (p. 267), confirming her symbolic intent with respect to the employment of the bay.

Beryl, whose main complaint in "Prelude" is that she is isolated from life, imprisoned in the new house in the suburbs, exposes herself (literally) to the dangers of life at the water's edge. Mrs. Harry Kember and her husband (reminiscent of Face and Mug in "Bliss" in their underlying similarities) act as the agents of seduction as they seek to involve the young and innocent Beryl in the sordid activities of morally unscrupulous adults. Ironically, the freedom of action for which Beryl has longed turns out to be more restrictive an imprisonment for the impressionable girl than the previous isolation. Though she goes with Harry freely, "the shadows were like iron bars." She must break free from Harry's grasp as she senses the unwholesomeness of the role which in fancy she has long coveted. Implicitly, the point is made that the price of immersion in the destructive waters is high, but growing old, a withered spinster in a mackintosh, is worse.

Mansfield saves the most explicit treatment of the motif of freedom and imprisonment for Jonathan Trout, whose life as a clerk circumscribes his freedom for "eleven months and a week" (p. 291) each year. In his own terms, he is worse than a prisoner of the state, for he wills his own imprisonment. He is an insect flying frantically about a room and doing "everything on God's earth, in fact, except fly out again" (p. 292). But a rule of mankind prevents him from breaking out of his imprisonment. He will continue to circle his prison as long as he lives, never taking advantage of the opportunity, always physically present, to escape. Perhaps his attitude here explains Jonathan's change of mood earlier as he emerges from the water of life and freedom to begin another day of hapless imprisonment:

> But now he was out of the water Jonathan turned blue with cold. He ached all over; it was as though some one was wringing the blood out of him. And stalking up the beach, shivering, all his muscles tight, he too felt his bathe was spoilt. He'd stayed in too long. (pp. 267–68)

As though to cap the motif, Mansfield writes section eight, recording a visit of Alice, the servant girl, to Mrs. Stubbs. The late Mr. Stubbs is described as having been carried off by dropsy, and his wife supplies the detail that an accumulation of liquid in his body hastened his end. Rather than mourning his passing, however, Mrs. Stubbs shocks Alice by insisting cheerily that "freedom's best" (p. 287).

If "Prelude" is an annunciation of birth, with just enough of death (the decapitation of the duck) to lend perspective to the human situation, "At the Bay" seems dramatically to reverse these two prime elements. The boy has been born and, a real flesh-and-blood creature in the garden, ceases to be a mystery. The reader sees him only briefly, but in that fleeting scene the infant is learning, like Wordsworth's darling of a pigmy size, to adjust to the world. He makes an enormous effort and turns over. In this story, however, the emphasis is on the decline of the human condition and the slope toward death. For Kezia, it is the momentary recognition that, like Uncle William, both she and Grandmother must eventually die. For Beryl, it is the end of innocence and romance, the beginning of the knowledge that comes with maturity. For the grandmother, it is the realization of the short span remaining to her in the world. To Stanley, though he is probably too obtuse to recognize the implications, the birth of his son, the male who will supplant him in the next generation, signals the onset of his own decline. Most obviously in Jonathan, whose parting words to his sister are "I'm old—I'm old" (p. 294), the momentum toward decline is demonstrated. In face he calls attention to his silvering hair, which in Mansfield's words is "like the breast plumage of a black fowl" (p. 294). The reader wonders whether one is to make reference to the death of the duck in "Prelude" as foreshadowing. Finally, in Linda's musings in the garden on the dropping of the blossoms from the trees, the motif of senseless fecundity ending in wasteful loss is verbalized:

But as soon as they flowered, they fell and were scattered. You brushed them off your frock as you talked. . . . Why, then, flower at all? Who takes the trouble—or the joy—to make all these things that are wasted, wasted. (p. 278)

Perhaps the differing emphases in the two stories result from the artist's desire to balance birth and death, rise and fall, the poles of existence. More likely, however, the change of stress is at least partially accounted for by Mansfield's own growing realization that the hopes she had harbored in 1916, as she wrote "Prelude," were impossible of fulfillment. By the time she came to compose "At the Bay," in 1921 the realization that "hope comes to die" was strong. The immanency of her own fate depressed her to the point of breakdown. In penetrating to the core of life to show its beauty, Mansfield could not avoid also showing its sadness.

John Middleton Murry's publication of Mansfield's early version of "The Prelude" in 1930 under the title of *The Aloe* [21] has afforded readers of Mansfield's fiction an unusual opportunity to observe the artist at work. In the short space of a year, she had learned much about technique and she proceeded to turn a good narrative into a tight and artistically sound short story. Sylvia Berkman, in her critical study of Mansfield, has devoted a great many pages to detailed treatment of the changes wrought from one draft to the other, concentrating her efforts mainly on the alterations made to the characters, especially the depiction of Linda Burnell.

The changes brought about by Mansfield's increasing mastery of her medium are even more interesting. The four major divisions of *The Aloe*, each with a fixed title, give way to the twelve more fluid parts of "Prelude." It is as though the author has discovered that life is not, in Virginia Woolf's image, a series of gig-lamps symmetrically arranged, but more a luminous halo. The twelve parts can be justified in themselves, but the effect of increasing the artificial divisions is less to fragment the whole than to allow the pieces of mosaic to form patterns effortlessly.

The Aloe is longer than "Prelude," long enough to

have been published by Knopf as a book of 135 pages. Part of its greater bulk is attributable to narrative material included in the former that Mansfield excludes from the latter. *The Aloe* contains an extended description of Mrs. Trout, the sister of Linda and Beryl, who has no role in the later version. The Samuel Josephs family is similarly given background treatment omitted from "Prelude." Instead of offering the long description of the general store at which Kezia and Lottie stop on their way to the new house, "Prelude" has the girls fall asleep on the journey and wake up upon arrival at the new place. The most extensive deletion from the early to the later version concerns Linda's father, his character, their relationship, and his attitude to the courting of his daughter by young Stanley Burnell. Touches remain of this phase of Linda's development in "Prelude," but full expository treatment is missing.

All these major omissions from "Prelude" seem artistically justifiable—and, all except the last, inevitable. Though *The Aloe* presents Mrs. Trout as a wholly identifiable character, it does not make a case for necessarily including her in the story. Rather than sharpening the rivalry and tension between Beryl and Linda, if anything, the presence of Mrs. Trout blurs the relationship of the other two. As for the delineation of the Samuel Josephs family, it might have made an excellent story of its own but it hardly contributes anything to the vision of life presented through the Burnells and their everyday activities. Similarly, eliminating the scene which Lottie and Kezia observe at the store in *The Aloe* takes nothing meaningful away from "Prelude," and merely removes a possible extrusion from the narrative.

Mansfield's decision to eliminate all but a suggestion of the relationship between Linda and her father may have been a mistake. In "Prelude," the reader realizes that the importance to her of the memory of her father is greater than he, as reader, has been prepared for. He does not understand why Linda should be in the presence of her father during the dream sequence and why it should be her father rather than Pat, for instance, who points out the bird to her. Had the role of the father been allowed to remain as prominent as it is in *The Aloe*, a certain amount of mystification would have been eliminated. This assumes, of course, that the author wished to make the relationship clear—a consideration not at all certain.

In fact, many of the omissions from "Prelude" appear designed to render the theme less immediately obvious than it was in *The Aloe*, as Joyce's "The Sisters" becomes less and less naturalistic as the artist's skill advances. Thus, Mrs. Trout's fantasies are in part taken over by Linda in the later version. If "Prelude" is about life and death, ostensibly Mansfield did not want too stark a statement of woman's role in the process. Mrs. Trout is not allowed to intrude her fear of dying in childbirth or of losing her child in the process. Nor is she permitted to fantasize the death of Grandmother Fairfield in the conflagration of the new house, called Tarana in *The Aloe*. The death of the old lady will be prefigured, but subtly, in the sequel to "Prelude," later on. Other examples of details that would support the theme of "Prelude" but that are omitted from it perhaps because their directness of expression inhibits the development of the story by suggestion and symbol are easy to find. In *The Aloe*, this passage appears:

> The old woman sighed and lay down beside her. Kezia thrust her head under the Grandmother's arm.
>
> "Who am I?" she whispered. This was an old established ritual to be gone through between them.
>
> "You are my little brown bird," said the Grandmother. (p. 38)

Here the grandmother is the mother hen, quite obviously, sheltering and giving identity to the chick under her wing, and Kezia is called directly a bird, another allusion reinforcing the motif of birds so prominent in both stories. In the same vein, the birth of Kezia is openly described in the early story, suppressed in the later. "Kezia had been born in that room. She had come forth squealing out of a reluctant mother in the teeth of a 'Southerly Buster' " (p. 15). Perhaps wisely, Mansfield decided to soften the impact of the motif of birth, motherhood, sex, and death in favor of a technique of understatement and suggestion.

Less easily explicable is Mansfield's alteration of the character and role of Nan Pym in the story from the early version to "Prelude." In *The Aloe* Beryl recalls her friend sharply and unambiguously as a pervert, a lesbian, who "would snatch up Beryl's hair and bury her face in it, and kiss it, or clasp her hands round Beryl's head and press it back against her firm breast" (p. 130). At such moments Beryl responds with "a violent thrill of physical dislike" and does not try to "suppress her contempt and her disgust" (pp. 130–31). In "Prelude," Nan is hardly a character at all—merely a name as the addressee of the letter Beryl composes. The reader knows little more about her than that "men were not at all keen on Nan, who was a solid kind of girl, with fat hips and a high colour (p. 261).

Why Mansfield drew back from her original presentation of Nan is difficult to say. The tone of "Prelude" is muted, and the emphasis is on the everyday normal development of ordinary people. The original delineation of Nan may have seemed too jarring and ugly for the idyll to sustain. Like the cats in Bertha's garden in "Bliss," Nan in Beryl's bedroom is a trifle too "creepy." Bertha must be aroused from her dream world in the course of her story while the assault on Beryl's dreamy innocence must await her experience with the Harry Kembers in "At the Bay." Whatever else the title "Prelude" signifies, it indicates a period before fulfillment through experience of the world and, in that sense, ought to exclude the kind of direct confrontation with sordid awareness that Nan's acts involve.

The specific verbal changes introduced by Mansfield from one draft to the next are as interesting to note as the omissions. As the considerably shorter "Prelude" would suggest, many of the changes involve rewriting to give tautness and concision to the revised text. " 'Do stars ever blow about?' she [Kezia] asked" in both versions. In *The Aloe,* the storeman answers, "Well, I never *noticed* 'em" (p. 24). In "Prelude," his response is simply and colloquially, "Not to notice" (p. 225). This is typical of the pruning process. In like fashion, adjectives and adverbs tend to disappear in "Prelude," such frequent words as "very" and "big" having been eliminated wholesale along the way.

The greatest number of verbal alterations move in the direction of increased descriptive precision, generally involving a change from an abstract word or phrase to a more vivid evocation of a sense impression. Mansfield moves, in fact, from the counters of expository prose to the language of poetry. For instance, a "charming gesture" in *The Aloe* becomes a "languid gesture" in "Prelude." The early version describes Lottie and Kezia as they "lay down back to back, just touching, and fell asleep" (p. 35). In the revision, this becomes, "And then they lay down back to back, their little behinds just touching, and fell asleep" (p. 229). In *The Aloe,* Beryl's breath rises and falls like "fairy wings," but they become "fanning" wings later on. In the first draft, the reader sees Stanley giving himself "a good scratch before turning in" (p. 36). The later version focuses the picture by localizing the scratch to "his shoulders and back" (p. 230). The first attempt shows Stanley "saturated with health" (p. 41), while the later paragraph describes him as "delighted with his firm, obedient body" (p. 232).

In her revision of *The Aloe,* Mansfield apparently gained confidence too that she could control the point of view of her story so that she might eliminate many of the explanatory "thought Kezia" or "reflected Linda" attributions that lend awkwardness to parts of *The Aloe.* In the early version, Mansfield begins a paragraph containing about two hundred words with the following: "But no, Kezia had seen a bull through a hole in a knot of wood in the high paling fence that separated the tennis lawn from the paddock" (p. 68). The final sentence of the paragraph reads: "The little paths were wet and clayey with tree roots spanned across them, 'like big fowls' feet,' thought Kezia" (p. 68). Substantially the same paragraph in "Prelude" ends with the word "feet" (pp. 238–39). Nor is there any need on the reader's part for reassurance that he is still dealing at the end with Kezia's consciousness. In this respect, though close together in time of composition, the later version is considerably more "modern" than the earlier.

4

Man and Woman

More than she apparently realized, Mansfield's stories are involved with the life she led and the people she knew best. Occasionally the identification with autobiographical incidents and people is openly acknowledged. "Prelude" and "At the Bay" were to be celebrations of her family in their New Zealand environment. Other stories involving the Burnell family (in various easily pierced disguises) are clearly in this vein. At times, in her letters she explains that this or that character bears a deliberate resemblance to a member of the Mansfield-Murry circle, though in editing Mansfield's papers, her husband usually omits the name of the individual so identified.

The stories in which she seems most emotionally involved, however, ordinarily appear to soften the urgency of involvement by giving the impression of being about characters far removed from the orbit of the writer and her immediate circle. If identification is made elsewhere of the dramatis personae, the similarity to the persons named seems merely superficial and convenient to the careful reader, though he must often believe that Mansfield believes utterly that she is telling the truth in her letters.

In actuality, as she describes the relationship between man and woman, Mansfield seems incapable of putting out of her mind her own all-pervasive involvement with John Middleton Murry.[1] Her fiction, therefore, becomes a multifaceted examination of the Mansfield-Murry relationship as ideally it might have been; as in its worst aspects it was; at it might have developed given a series of alternative routes to fulfillment; as it might have been had the woman been different; had the man been different; had the times allowed. The relationship is examined in caricature, in dream, in dramatic form, and otherwise until its obsessive character is quite plain. It is not surprising that Mansfield wrote Murry, though apparently in jest: "And now, of course, I see future generations finding you in all my books: 'the man she was in love with!' "[2]

It is instructive to examine three stories written at scattered intervals after Mansfield's relationship with Murry began, from "Something Childish But Very Natural" (1914) to "Je ne parle pas français" (1918) to "The Man Without a Temperament" (1920) in order to see the widely different ways in which the relationship could be viewed and approached by the woman involved who was also the artist recording the affair.

That the relationship was at the core of Mansfield's entire adult emotional life is beyond question. Nor is it morbidly strange that her private reactions to their love should have poured over into all the fiction she conceived, for there was nowhere else it could go. Deprived of Murry's physical presence for all but a few months of their decade of involvement, she let her physical need and psychological deprivation find outlet in fictional projections. Like Keats again, Mansfield in her exiled misery, with full knowledge of the infectious and probably fatal nature of her disease, had to seek relief in fantasy and in the contrivance of her fiction. All male protagonists became for her, probably often without her being conscious of it, aspects of her husband; all heroines possible surrogates for herself. What she does with these surrogates is interesting.

"Something Childish But Very Natural" is the story of an idyllic love affair involving two childern in their middle teens, a dream idyll of sensitive emotional involvement in a hazy world that excludes all but the two lovers. "It's people that make things so—silly. As long as you can keep away from them you're safe and you're happy" (p. 172). The youngsters meet on a train and, after clumsy preliminaries, draw close to one another. Except for the fact that Edna will not allow Henry to touch her, even to put his arm around her, their joy is complete. All Edna can say to explain her insistence on keeping her distance is that after contact "We wouldn't be children any more" (p. 175). They find the cottage of their dreams in the country and actually let it from the owner. Then, while waiting for Edna to arrive so that they can begin their life of playing at being householders, Henry falls asleep and dreams of a little girl delivering a telegram to him at the gate.

One need not speculate on the identity of the two principals. The early letters of Mansfield to Murry abound with references to their child-love. "We are two shining children leaning over that arc of light and looking down undaunted." [3] "My love, my child playfellow," [4] she calls him in another letter. They are "like two little children who have been turned out into the garden," [5] and she likes the new sensation so much that "this grown up world everywhere *don't* fit me" [6] anymore. In another letter, she and Murry are "children"—"aliens and strangers in this world." [7] In still another, she says, "I feel we are about fifteen today—just children." [8]

But the lovers of the story share a paradise of dreamlike innocence forever closed to the more sophisticated author and her lover. From the first, Edna is associated with gardens and with Eden in particular. Even Edna's name is almost an anagram for Eden. She and Henry, like Adam and Eve, are in a world of their own. Their happiness, according to the girl, is dependent on their remaining innocent children and hence her unwillingness to know him physically. The story is replete with references to her "marigold hair" (p. 178), and to her gathering primroses. Their being together is said to be as natural as "trees or birds or clouds" (p. 178). There is even a scene in which she leads him to a bower where the lovers can engage in amorous dalliance (p. 179). Her green coat and her hat with a wreath upon it confirm her flowery connections, while her eyebrows, like "feathers," give her birdlike characteristics. As if to complement this amalgam of nature, Henry describes his own eager eyes as "two drunken bees" (p. 166). It is almost hyperbolic that in the garden of the dream cottage that they let, the trees are apple trees, and, what's more, they are "full of angels" (p. 181). "Evening light," it seems, "is awfully deceptive" (p. 181). If anything, Mansfield is trying too hard here to reinforce the Eden motif, the theme of unspoiled natural love, surrounded by a sullied, ugly, unlovely environment from which only the intensity of their innocent love can save them.

Mansfield's problem as a storyteller (and perhaps as a woman too) is that a love of such intense and idyllic dimensions cannot be sustained in an enclave within a hostile world—except, of course, in the dream world of the imagination. But the problem is for her, as it was for Keats in some poems, its own solution. Invest the love experience with the quality of dream and leave it to the reader to suspend willingly whatever portion of his disbelief the narrative invites. Put the events in the half-world between dream and waking, between heaven and earth, between light and darkness, between fact and fancy.

Selecting this method, Mansfield introduces through Henry's reverie at the beginning of the story a poem called "Something Childish But Very Natural" (p. 165), in which the speaker wishes he were a "feathery" bird and could fly to his love. Being human, however, he must remain where he is. Therefore he must be with his beloved only in sleep and dream, a fine situation if not for the fact that waking proves him to be alone again. Yet to wake is unavoidable but bearable only if the lover can shut his eyes in the dark and dream on. Henry's comment on the poem is that the poet "wrote it when he was half-awake some time, for it's got a smile of a dream on it" (p. 166). Just as the story ends, Henry thinks again of the lines of the poem:

> Had I two little wings,
> And were a little feathery bird,
> To you I'd fly, my dear (p. 182),

and he proceeds forthwith to fall asleep and dream of the little girl with the telegram for him. The story ends:

> The garden became full of shadows—they span a web of darkness over the cottage and the trees and Henry and the telegram. But Henry did not move. (p. 183)

Within the frame of the poem and the dream, the love relationship is pictured, and the affair depends upon the dream just as much as the love of Madeline and Porphyro does in "The Eve of St. Agnes." Mansfield presents the meetings of the lovers as from a great distance, through the wrong end of the telescope. The lovers become archetypes, bigger (or perhaps smaller) than life, but certainly not real people partaking of the life of London and its suburbs. One knows that they have families, but one cannot imagine the lives of these protagonists within their family circles. Rather they are are at home, as already said, with butterflies, flowers, bees, clouds, and gardens, apart from worldly associations.

Henry, for instance, is portrayed as beyond the call of this world. Illusion and reality are for him difficult to separate. He is "a great fellow for books" (p. 165). Immersed in reverie, he almost misses his train. He is not sure at times if the words that come into his mind are his own or whether he had seen them in a book. He fantasizes their life together in the dream cottage, and he feels that "if you listen to a kettle right through it's like an early morning in Spring" (p. 176). The scene in the wood raises the motif of the dream life to a crescendo. Henry is "full of dreams," and "ever since waking he had felt so strangely that he was not really awake at all, but just dreaming. The time before, Edna was a dream and now he and she were dreaming together and somewhere in some dark place another dream waited for him" (p. 178). The sense of unreality becomes so strong that he asks, "Are we a dream?" (p. 178).

The pattern is almost symmetrical. As Henry subdues his worldly passions to enter wholeheartedly into a love of blissful, dreamy innocence, his beloved throws off her reservations concerning the physical and shows Henry that she now desires him. At this point the narrative breaks off, to resume at a later time with Henry in possession of the dream cottage waiting for the arrival of Edna. His thoughts are of their anticipated life together during the evening to come, surprisingly undreamy details of having supper, changing their candles, and retiring to their separate rooms. Perhaps the actuality exerts a sobering influence upon him, for, obviously recalling Keats's "Ode to a Grecian Urn," he decides that there is no hurry for her arrival—"because the waiting is a sort of Heaven, too, darling" (p. 182). Now comes the sleep and the real dream.

The ending—often called the least effective part of

this story—is capable of many interpretations. The "big white moth" that turns out to be "a little girl in a pinafore" (p. 182) may well be his dream projection of Edna. Edna has previously been associated with white more than once: Henry brings her white pinks, the woman at the cottage offers her white jonquils, and throughout her role as child-lover and symbol of purity is emphasized. Certainly the fact that the character is a little girl fits the impression of Edna that the author has been seeking to paint. Even the notion that the small child is a moth—Henry's first impression—is consistent with Mansfield's frequent use of that insect as symbolically an innocent human being attracted by the bright spots of this world and thus trapped in the prison house of existence, with early death the only way out. The world is cruel to moths in "At the Bay" and Jonathan Trout is quick to point out the implications for himself in the fate of the insects.

The dream itself is by definition unreal, but even within that dream the dreamer is conscious of one illusion after the other. Nothing is what it seems to be. The girl seems a moth but is found to be a girl. The telegram she gives him is found not to be a telegram at all—"just a folded paper" (p. 183). It *is* only a "make-believe one" but it does not have "one of those snakes inside that fly up at you" (p. 182). In every instance, the dreamer is made aware that things are not as they seem at first to be. As he realizes this in the dream,

> The garden became full of shadows—they span a web of darkness over the cottage and the trees and Henry and the telegram. But Henry did not move. (p. 183)

The possibilities of interpretation are considerable. The reader may hark back to the closing lines of the "Something Childish" poem, which tell of the lover awakening in the morning before dawn and, still in darkness though awake, dreaming on. If one looks at the ending in this way, the story ends on an upward curve, Henry awaiting his beloved in the garden in anticipatory joy.

Such an interpretation, however, is unlikely in terms of the imagery employed. The probable significance of the little girl as a dream-equivalent of Edna has been mentioned, as has the association of this girl with a moth. The fact that she bears a telegram is interesting, for Mansfield in her letters places the receipt of telegrams very high on her list of significant happenings. She often implores her lover to send a telegram in order to reassure her that all is well, and with scandalous extravagance she often sends Murry telegrams when the emotional need to communicate is urgent. In the story, the telegram is first thought to be "make-believe," and to contain a cardboard snake. The use of the snake image in the context of gardens and Edens here seems deliberate—a hint of the end of the idyll, of the intrusion of corrupt world outside on the lovers. In a sense, furthermore, the discovery that the sheet is not a telegram at all but "just a folded paper" is even more dismaying than the idea that it contained a snake as a practical joke. Indeed, the lack of a message, the failure of the little girl's paper to communicate anything, *is* the joke, *is* the end of relationship between the dream lovers as prefigured, appropriately, in a dream. The way in which this foreshadowing will eventually be brought to actuality is left to the imagination: Edna's possible failure to arrive, the arrival of a real telegram that fails to communicate any meaningful message, and so on. The precise way is unimportant. Yet it is hard to mistake the ironic difference between the darkness described in the little poem and the darkness that envelops Henry now. In the poem it is the darkness just before dawn; here it is the darkness of evening—the end of the day.

The garden is "full of shadows," promising greater darkness to follow in the garden that earlier had been clothed in bright radiance. To cap her intent, Mansfield reveals that the shadows "span a web of darkness" over everything. In 1918, speaking of herself and Murry, Mansfield wrote in a letter to her husband: "The great thing for these two children to do is to go slow . . . hold hands . . . not walk into spider's webs and always have a small sit-down before they decide to walk into parlours—see?" [9] The darkness of the garden is obviously not something desirable, and Henry, unmoving, seems a dead and frozen figure in the last line, a fitting attitude for him to assume now that he is to be metaphorically cast out of the garden.

To adduce all the relevant biographical resemblances between the details of Mansfield's life with Murry and the fictional relationship of Edna and Henry would require a great deal of space. Mansfield's consistent reference to the two of them as children has already been recorded. It is well known that for years Mansfield kept before herself the dream cottage (they called it "The Heron") that she and Murry would find and live in with euphoric disregard of the world about them.[10] In fact, one of the most pitiful of Mansfield's letters, which describes her ultimate realization that this cottage would remain merely a symbol ever unattained in actuality, is not far from stating the theme of "Something Childish." At the same time, both Murry and Mansfield, in their letters, depict vividly their discovery of several real cottages (like the Villa Pauline) and their ecstatic efforts to adorn them for occupancy by the lovers when the absent one shall have been reunited with the one on the spot. Just as Henry rehearses in his mind all the commonplace details of an evening together, so Mansfield in her letters describes every detail of her next projected meeting with Murry.

The similarities of the protagonists to Mansfield and Murry are less actual than they are psychological and spiritual. When they met, neither the young critic nor his story-writing friend were innocent of the world or of sexual experimentation as Henry and Edna apparently are. Their innocence lay in the attitude they adopted toward their human relationship—the care they took to nurture what was pure and straight in their unconventional mode of life. There is no reason to doubt that both of them, in letters and in private papers, believe completely in the purity of the association, quite as much as they believe in the ugliness and corruption of the world outside their garden.

If there is falsification in "Something Childish But Very Natural," perhaps it lies in the apparent transfer of roles from female to male. The story is told from the point of view of Henry, a minor tour de force in itself when carried off successfully by a feminine writer who must invest the male character with a full set of thoughts and feelings that the authoress, as a woman, can never have had in precisely the same way. Perhaps the attempt is somewhat less than successful here, for Henry, as commentators on the stories have noted, emerges as a very feminine character, effusive, ecstatic, unconvincing in his extruded maleness. That he, rather than Edna, bears the weight of Mansfield's personality more than of Murry's is extremely likely; as Ursula in Lawrence's *The Rainbow* is more Lawrence than she is any female person its author ever knew. In real life, it was Mansfield who, more often than not, found quarters for herself and Murry and who awaited his coming with trembling anticipation. And it was he, more often than not, who was prevented from arriving. Factually, it was Mansfield who suggested first their living together and afterward the physical relationship from which Murry at first shrank.[11] In a revelatory entry in her *Scrapbook*, dated December 17,

1919, Mansfield herself comments on their real-life reversal of roles:

We had been *children* to each other, openly confessed children, telling each other everything, and each depending equally upon the other. *Before that, I had been the man and he had been the woman* [italics mine], and he had been called upon to make no real efforts. He had never really "supported" me. When we first met, in fact, it was I who kept him. . . . Then this illness, getting worse and worse, and turning me into a woman. . . . He stood it marvellously. It helped very much because it was a "romantic" disease (his love of a "romantic appearance" is *immensely* real) and also being "children" together gave us a practically unlimited chance to play at life—not to live. It was child love.[12]

In his autobiography, too, Murry agrees that he was in his early relationship with Mansfield "a strange creature. Assuredly, there was little indeed of the conquering male about me." [13] He goes on at length, in words that Edna might have used, but not the Henry of the story, to explain his position:

Anyhow, it is true that I did not want to be Katherine's lover. Or if I did, I was unconscious that I did. And the way I suppressed my unconscious desire, if it needed suppressing, was to be very clear and positive, as I was, that sex spoiled love. . . . It was marvelous to me to have Katherine as my companion. I could talk to her intimately in a way I had never talked to anyone before. We trusted one another. . . . We were on the threshold of a new country.[14]

It is clear from these extended passages that Murry's views and feelings are closer to those of the girl in the story, Mansfield's closer to the male protagonist. What is not clear is why Mansfield chose to execute the story in this way: whether it offered more of a challenge technically to reverse the sexes and the roles; whether there is an element of wish fulfillment at work in the dream atmosphere of the fiction; or whether, since Edna in the story advances from her original frigidity while Henry withdraws into acceptable passivity, Mansfield is attempting to find a common ground, through manipulation, where male and female can meet.

John Middleton Murry sees in "Je ne parle pas français" a great short story but "there is also a moving personal symbolism:

> The fate of the Mouse, caught in the toils of the world's evil, abandoned by her lover, is Katherine's fate.[15]

He reiterates that "the Mouse *is* Katherine, the secret Katherine, the Katherine whom I alone knew, and the world never can. Mysteriously, unconsciously, she had spoken a doom."[16] By this time, four years after "Something Childish," it will be noted that the roles have reversed themselves to the normal and that it is the man who abandons the waiting woman, not Edna who fails to keep her appointment with Henry. By this time, too, Mansfield has progressed technically and personally to the point at which the lovers and their affair are deliberately presented to the reader not as one sees the other and himself, but, significantly, through the corrupt eyes and sensibility of the degenerate world outside, through, incidentally, a third-party narrator who in his overt effeminacy and probable homosexuality, combines the male and female characteristics that Mansfield tried to place differently in the earlier story.

Mansfield herself was not aware, it would seem, of the degree to which her own situation paralleled that of Mouse—nor did she realize that Dick Harmon's actions resulted in the same fate for the young woman as Murry's seemed likely to produce in her own life. In her letter to Murry of February 4, 1918, she reports on the background of the story:

It needs perhaps some explanation. The subject, I mean *lui qui parle,* is of course taken from———and———[deletions made by Murry as editor of *Letters*], and God knows who. It has been more or less in my mind ever since I first felt strongly about the French. . . .

There's so much less taken from life than anybody would credit. The African laundress I had a bone of—but only a bone—Dick Harmon, of course is, partly is———[the final dash is Mansfield's, but it is illogical that she would break off at this point if Murry himself had been the one in her mind.].

In the same lettter, she reveals her concern with the judgment of the story, admitting that in it she had "bitten deeper and deeper and deeper than ever I have before." [17]

The portrait of Dick Harmon and Mouse that emerges from the story is too familiar for the resemblance to be accidental. Harmon is the tweedy Englishman abroad, a writer and critic, sophisticated and withdrawn at parties, gazing at life with a dreamy smile. Attractive to women, "all the time we were together Dick never went with a woman. I sometimes wondered whether he wasn't completely innocent" (p. 361). His return to Paris in the company of Mouse finds him nervous, haggard, out of his depth, as he attempts to book two rooms in a hotel for him and his companion. His eventual flight from Mouse and the uncongenial environment, abandoning his love in the nightmare hotel room (a far cry from the abandonment of Henry in the garden of the dream cottage), is one of Mansfield's constant fears with regard to the future of her relationship with Murry.

The description of Mouse in certain important respects recalls the portrait of Edna in "Something Childish." The narrator's first view of her is as she emerges from a train and walks through the railroad station. "Not this *baby* [italics mine] walking beside the old porter as though he were her nurse" (p. 366). She is "beautiful," "exquisite," "fragile," "fine." She is a "tiny creature, half butterfly, half woman" (p. 368). Her long lashes are topped by eyebrows that look like "two little feathers" (p. 358). Again the girl is made to resemble creatures of the garden, butterflies and birds. And the fur of her muff and coat collar and cuffs suggests an animal quality "carrying out the mouse idea" (p. 368). When, suspecting Harmon's defection and flight, she returns without him from his bedroom, this butterfly-mouse creature carries a letter with her and, in a trancelike state, drops it on the floor. The elements of the end of "Something Childish" are here repeated with a difference. The abandoned party receives a letter from her lover. Instead of a moth-creature who turns out to be a little girl in a pinafore bearing a telegram, there is a butterfly-mouse creature, this time the addressee, who reads the words in a dream. Even the mention of her "spidery handwriting" (p. 375) in the letter recalls the "web" of darkness spun for Henry at the end of the other story, for Mouse is the spider into whose web Harmon had stumbled in terms of the conflicting demands made upon him by the oedipal attraction to his mother and his affection for the girl. In the present story, Mouse is the victim of a double abandonment, for Dick's desertion is followed by Duquette's duplicity.

In order to stress the relationship of the story to several of Mansfield's other pieces of fiction, and the resemblances of characters in it to Mansfield and Murry, it has been necessary to distort Mansfield's real accomplishment in "Je ne parle pas français." Her sudden ability to create a Dostoyevskian protagonist and narrator from whose corrupted point of view the Harmon-Mouse affair might be commented upon frightened the author herself and is a source of amazement to critics. To realize that this story was written almost at the same time as the slight and frivolous "Sun and Moon" is to wonder all the more at the psychic energy and the burst of creative inspiration that went into the shaping and executing of Mouse's story. It seems inescapable that the story obsessed its creator primarily because of her own perhaps unconscious involvement in it. Murry saw this too: "Here you seem to have begun to drag *the depths of your consciousness.* . . . the world is shut out. You are looking into yourself." [18] And Mansfield admits that the story arises from "an *extremely* deep sense of hopelessness, of everything doomed to disaster." She calls it finally "*a cry against corruption.*" [19] In this respect, Murry is wrong to say that the world is "shut out." It is the world's corruption—from Harmon's relationship to his mother, on the one hand, to Duquette's relationship to his African laundress—that renders the plight of Mouse so hopeless. Abandoned by both men, certain of rejection by the people back home and of exploitation by the Frenchmen around her (as Mansfield believed she herself was),[20] Mouse can only huddle in her coat and keep her hands in her fur muff while she tries to avoid contact with a soiled environment.

"The Man Without a Temperament" exhibits the same materials as are found in the other two stories—but the tone, the point of view, and the treatment are quite different. Again the focus is on a man and a woman in an intimate relationship. Once more abandonment underlies the narrative, though in this story neither the man nor the woman is physically abandoned. And once more it seems obvious that Mansfield draws the details of the story from her life with Murry.

The period immediately surrounding the writing of the story is well documented and explains a great deal concerning the heaviness and hopelessness of the mood. Very sick by this time (1920), with the realization that she had not too long to live, still separated from her husband for long periods, while he worked to support them in London and she sought the more congenial climate of southern Europe, Mansfield came as close to bitterness as she ever approached during the years with Murry. Though she could understand logically the necessity for him to remain with his editorial work in London, she could no longer accept emotionally being deprived of the solace of the only human being whose presence she needed. Correspondence was proving to be less satisfactory than it had formerly been. Numbering each letter until the distant date of their next reunion had ceased to be an exhilarating game. As her life ebbed, Mansfield wanted fulfillment now.

The verbal result of this new bitterness is the poem, "The New Husband," now printed in her *Scrapbook* (December 8, 1919) and originally sent in a letter to Murry.[21] The poem is a succinct, harsh, straightforward statement of her intention to transfer her affections to an unnamed "New Husband" who will be physically close to her, who will not plead the necessity to extend his period of absence for practical reasons, who will be tender, solicitous, loving, and, most important, always there at her side. Much of the poem is taken up with describing her present husband's actions and motivations as a contrast to those of the hypothetical new spouse.

> Who's your man [says the new suitor] to leave you be
> Ill and cold in a far country?
> Who's the husband—who's the stone
> Could leave a child like you alone?
> You're like a leaf caught in the wind;
> You're like a lamb that's left behind
> When all the flock has pattered away;
> You're like a pitiful little stray
> Kitten that I'd put in my vest;
> You're like a bird that's fallen from nest.
>
> We've none of us too long to live,
> Then take me for your man and give

Me all the keys to all your fears
And let me kiss away these tears.

. . . .

I thought with grief upon that other [Murry];
But then why should he ought discover
Save that I pined away and died?
So I became the stranger's bride.

The receipt of this poem in the mail so shook Murry that he left immediately for Mansfield's side.

"The Man Without a Temperament" is a quietly passionate projection of the possible outcome of their relationship—the woman becomes the jailer, her husband the prisoner, in a hellish charade of marital fidelity and companionship. The fly in the ointment is the complete absence of any emotional bonds between the two in the present or hope of any future bonds. Only the flashbacks to the past furnish evidence of what might have been. Though hardly ever out of her husband's sight or deprived of his overweening care, she is as surely abandoned as Mouse or Henry in the earlier stories.

The story is properly the most sober, mature, and realistic of the three. The dream atmosphere of "Something Childish" has given way to an objective matter-of-fact recital of days and nights in a hotel on the Italian Riviera. The lush youth of Henry and Edna is replaced by the disillusioned maturity of Mr. Salesby and his invalid wife. The beautiful "baby" Mouse has been transformed into the ailing, fussy person Dick Harmon's mother may have been, and the demands on the husband are very much like the demands made on a son by a elderly and sickly mother. If there is any dream world left for the husband in the latest story, it lies in his memories of the dear dead days in London, now apparently difficult to recall.

As in the other two stories, though the presence of the woman is essential to the narrative, Mansfield focuses attention on the man and on his situation. The woman figure remains shadowy and insubstantial, as perhaps the author believes it in fact to be in a man's world. At the same time, in "The Man Without a Temperament," the frail, insubstantial, invalided wife keeps her more robust husband in virtual thralldom precisely through the weakness of her physique.

Mansfield's mastery of detail in this story calls for closer examination. It should be noted that the author surrounds her married couple with an assortment of other paired guests at the hotel. These pairs act deliberately in a variety of ways to accentuate the peculiar situation of the principal pair. Most obviously, the honeymoon couple intrudes to keep fresh in the mind of the reader—as of the husband Salesby—the sexual energy now dissipated in the pallid middle years of the protagonist couple. Their physical proximity, the perspiration that exudes from the wife, their fishing expedition, their glad animal movements contrast effectively with the measured aridity of the older couple. The Topknots, whose real names the the reader is not told, are a couple indistinguishable from one another (like the Face and Mug of "Bliss,") and may foreshadow the loss of individual identity of Mr. Salesby and his wife as their roles as jailer and jailed rob them of personal, identifiable characteristics in the view of outsiders. The Countess and the old General may be a projection into the future of the Salesby pair. The roles are reversed, but the picture of one looking after the other into senility is preserved:

> "The General's egg's too hard again."
> "Caw! Caw! Caw!" (p. 243)

Even the American woman and her cat "Klaymongso" are surely reminiscent of the Salesbys, for the woman considers the cat her protector and her playmate, much as the wife looks upon her husband.

Robert Salesby's role as servant is effectively highlighted by the presence in the story of the chambermaid and the waiter Antonio. The former realizes the status of the guest whose room she services and she looks at him with "impudent" eyes as she mocks him in his helplessness. The former is shown as a kind of guild brother of Robert. The wife sends Antonio off for tea as her needs impel her husband to go off on errands for her comfort. After delivering the mail to the couple, "Antonio wheeled sharply, stiffened, the grin went out of his face. His striped linen jacket and his flat gleaming fringe made him look like a wooden doll" (pp. 414–15). The implications are obvious. Just as Antonio is a paid servant, a puppet to be manipulated by the guests, so Robert is "a wooden doll" where his wife's needs are concerned. Always civil to her in her presence, like a well-conditioned butler, the symbolic grin goes out of his face too in those moments when he is temporarily free from his menial duties and no longer under observation. These latter moments are so infrequent, however, that he may truly be said to be a man without a temperament, borrowing as Antonio does a compliant and servile mask to fit the requirements of his mistress, in whatever mood he finds her.

If Salesby's wife is his mistress, she is even more his warder, and he is wholly imprisoned by the strength of her weakness. The pervasive imagery of the story is of entrapment. The most obvious reiterated action is Salesby's turning round and round on his finger the signet ring which he wears. This symbolic vestige of his lost identity as a person is visual evidence of his inability or unwillingness to break out of the circle of paralysis and immobility that his wife's demands have drawn around him. Pointed out as representing his imprisoned state by most critics of Mansfield, the ring is only one of many significant images. The elevator in the hotel is described as an "iron cage" (p. 413), and the reader is made to hear its iron gate clang open and shut more than once during the course of the story. In the dim lobby is a "black lattice" (p. 413) on which unclaimed letters are displayed—another hint of cages and bars. Meaningfully, the mosquito nettings of the bedspreads in their bedroom are referred to several times, and eventually one of the crucial scenes occurs inside the netting of the wife's bed. The wife's shawl is called "the grey cobweb" (p. 414), the third time, in the three stories under discussion here, that the suggestion of a spider's role is woven into the narrative.

Salesby's imprisonment is rendered the more intolerable by the taste of freedom afforded him in short and infrequent snatches. The three-quarters of an hour he allows himself for a walk alone is measured out for him by his wife as she watches the hands of his own timepiece. When he offers her his watch to consult in his absence, he is symbolically putting his time at her disposal—and she takes it eagerly. Mansfield notes that the watch Salesby hands over is "warm" p. 419), for it shares the heat of his body and is, obstensibly, to be equated with the gift to her of his entire existence.

What the wife cannot control is her husband's sorties into time past, when he was free, which he recalls in several flashbacks to their earlier life together in England. In these remembrances of things past, the entire tone alters, the tempo of the prose quickens, and the paralysis of the present is temporarily put aside until, in one of them, the present reasserts itself through the striking of a clock.

The final scene of the story, in which Salesby's wife asks him to kill a mosquito that has intruded beneath her netting is particularly significant. Obediently he lifts the net and destroys the insect, swollen with the blood of his wife perhaps, and then is invited to sit beneath the netting with his wife while she tests verbally his willingness to remain her prisoner. It would seem that, in one sense, the insect he kills is himself—the helpless creature imprisoned by the netting. On the other hand, to the degree that he has allowed his wife, as helpless though voracious parasite, to feed upon him, she may be identified with the dead mosquito and Salesby's action becomes a symbolic destruction of his wife. An imaginative reader may even find traces of Lady Macbeth's guilt at the murder of Duncan in Salesby's dipping his fingers in water to rid them of bloodstains; or traces of Othello's "Put out the light and then put out the light" in Salesby's final question: to his wife: "Shall I switch off the light?" (p. 425). It will be recalled that the line in *Othello* comes at the very moment of the strangling of the wife by her maddened husband. The ironically anticlimactic ending in which the wife asks Salesby whether he minds "awfully being out here with me" and is answered by the single word, "Rot" (p. 425), has been mentioned by most critics of the story. It is precisely the word to sum up the deadening, corrupting effect of Salesby's emotionally enforced imprisonment behind the net of his wife's needs. Though she is in the eyes of the world the invalid, the woman with the bad heart, actually it is Salesby who now has heart trouble, Salesby whose former strength has been sapped by the deadeningly artificial terms of the relationship. As the dust lays thick on the road leading from the hotel—as the deep valley reveals "a dried up river bed at the bottom" (p. 419)—so Salesby has been drained dry emotionally until he is a scarecrow to frighten little girls and make them run from their bathe. His inability to move, his rejection of the possibility of escape, the stagnation of a once-free human being are all epitomized in the final word that his lips whisper. Nor is it accidental that this monosyllable is whispered, not shouted. If we are to believe T. S. Eliot, this is indeed how Salesby's world ends.

Abandonment does not occur in "The Man Without a Temperament" as it does in the other two stories about man and woman. But spiritually and emotionally the wife of this story is more surely deserted than either of the other two principals. Henry has at the end at least the memory of something beautiful that was and the imaginative materials to create in fantasy what might have been. Cut off from Dick Harmon in the midst of their involvement, Mouse escapes the pain of seeing the gradual degeneration of love into something baser. But the Salesbys, *because* there is no real abandonment, must endure every minute and forever the patent and prolonged death of the heart which their relationship entails.

Mansfield's motivation for writing "The Man Without a Temperament" is not clear. In a way, it is the reverse side of the coin presented in her "The New Husband," in which she berates Murry for not being at her side when she needs him. But the bitter twist is that her imaginative projection of the opposite eventuality—Murry's faithful devotion to her in her exile and invalidism—is even worse than the separation she abhors. So the dream-fulfillment turns out to be a nightmare as Salesby performs the duties of nurse, servant, prisoner—but never of husband. Mansfield tells her Bogey (Boogles in the story) in a letter dated May 27, 1918:

> Our marriage. You cannot imagine what that was to have meant to me. It's fantastic—I suppose. It was to have shone—apart from all else in my life. And it really was only part of the nightmare, after all. You never once held me in your arms and called me your wife. . . . I had to keep on making you remember it.[22]

She recognizes in the same letter that her husband "has not this same devouring need for me that I have of him.

He *can* exist apart from me. . . . He will never realize that I am only WELL when we are 'together.' "[23]

Thus, the eternity for Mansfield from 1914 to 1920 turns the idealized romantic dream of Henry and Edna in "Something Childish But Very Natural" into the querulous complaint of a sick and disillusioned wife—strident though unspoken—over the dissipation of love. To keep one's lover physically on the scene is not enough, she finds. The trick is to keep the love as well. In its finality and hopelessness, "The Man Without a Temperament" is Mansfield's saddest story.

5

The Legacy of Fiction

"Bliss" is a story that illustrates Mansfield's mature ability to work simultaneously on several levels so that the finished product exhibits a richness of texture not ordinarily found in the English short story. At its most obvious, it is a psychological case study of an hysterical woman, Bertha Young, the kind of character sketch that the younger Mansfield experimented with in some of the stories of the *German Pension* volume. But by 1918 Katherine Mansfield had grown beyond the mere delineation of character as the primary objective of fiction. To complicate the picture and to ensure that her task as artist will not be "too easy," she restricts the point of view to Bertha's consciousness—a highly unreliable guide for the reader, who must evaluate all Bertha's impressions as to their basis in external reality or in the confused internal chaos of the woman's mind. Mansfield's ability through choice of words to have Bertha expose her psyche so that what is positive would seem to predominate while, at the same time, showing the negative aspects lurking beneath has been analyzed at length by Saralyn Daly in her *Katherine Mansfield.*[1] Beyond these aims, there is Mansfield's intention to work in a broad satire of the pseudo-sophisticated, brittle, superficial world of modern English "arty" circles. And finally, "Bliss" demonstrates its author's fascination with symbols employed to bring together diverse elements, to make the reader aware of meaningful ambiguities, and to provide cosmic overtones for people and events all too commonplace.

The title itself offers a hint of the ambivalences the story will encompass. Though at thirty, Bertha "Young" would seem to have very little to rejoice over, as the reader inspects the pattern of her life on the day the story depicts, yet Bertha identifies the state that grips her as "bliss," a state of heightened reaction to people and things. The mood calls for running, for bowling hoops, for throwing things into the air, for laughing uncontrollably, for trying to involve another human being in one's ecstasy—or at least for seeking to communicate one's mood to another. Yet the unconvinced reader feels that Bertha is closer to the point when she fears that she is "getting hysterical" (p. 339). Obviously (though not to Bertha) there is little to justify the bliss she insists she feels. Her relationship with her husband has apparently been largely unsucessful in spite of her extended rationalizations:

> Really—really—she had everything. She was young. Harry and she were as much in love as ever, and they got on together splendidly and were really good pals. She had an adorable baby. . . . And friends—modern, thrilling friends, writers and painters and poets or people keen on social questions. . . . and they were going abroad in the summer, and their new cook made the most superb omelettes. (p. 342)

The reader shortly discovers that the love has no sexual basis, that Bertha is "cold" (p. 348), that for the first time she "desired her husband" (p. 348) on this day, that her baby may be adorable but the control of the child has been usurped by the nurse so that Bertha must almost steal moments of affection when the nurse is busy at something else. And as for the "friends," even

Bertha admits on the night of the party that "they didn't share it" (p. 345), this bliss of hers that she finds so difficult to communicate.

The breathless ecstasy of the passage quoted above gives the lie to the words themselves. The twice-repeated "really" and the overenthusiastic "everything" reveal the emptiness of the lines. Being "in love" somehow is out of phase with being "really good pals." Nor do people who have "modern, thrilling friends, writers and painters and poets or people keen on social questions" speak or think about their friends in these stilted, unreal terms. Indeed, in a letter to Murry dated March 14, 1918, Mansfield explains that even Bertha realized "that those words and expressions were not and couldn't be hers. They were, as it were, *quoted* by her, borrowed with . . . an eyebrow." [2]

Mansfield then, over and over again, has Bertha insist upon her state of bliss while, in the very words which the author frames her insistence, she demonstrates the emptiness of the claims. It is, on the one hand, no wonder that Bertha fails to communicate to the others the feeling within her (since she misjudges it herself almost completely). And it is a question, on the other, whether the guests are not perhaps aware that Bertha's conduct does border on the hysterical—and are too polite to show their awareness of their hostess's emotional difficulties. Only in her strange relationship with Pearl Fulton does Bertha's bliss appear to be genuine; yet the intensity of her emotional involvement with Pearl seems neurotically unjustified and unmotivated.

The impossibility of verbally expressing true bliss is a major theme of the story. Bertha's party is a "talky" affair peopled by compulsive talkers like the Norman Knights and Eddie Warren. Harry is a loquacious person too, and only Bertha and Pearl say little although they feel much. Harry's only moment of bliss comes at parting from Pearl. Their appointment to meet again is made almost without words. Bertha's few moments of communion with little B. are likewise passed almost in silence even though the brief encounter is one of the high points of her day. The ironical fact that what is said is not nearly as significant as what is unsaid obviously is useful to the author in her role as social satirist as well, for it provides her with a means of channeling the extended and apparently haphazard conversation of these pseudo-bohemians to some purpose.

As the garden operates in "The Garden Party" to focus the reader's attention on what is meaningful in the midst of meaningless chatter, so the title "Bliss" works in this story. There is, of course, the old injunction that "Where ignorance is bliss 'Tis folly to be wise.' " Here, Bertha's breathless exhilaration is shown to be the result of her innocence of a relationship between Harry and Pearl. The implication is that when knowledge replaces unawareness at the end of the story, Bertha's bliss will be replaced by a new and more appropriate emotion. The garden itself makes its appearance again and functions much as it did for Laura. Bertha becomes, in this view, a more mature Eve than Laura, enjoying a wedded but platonic life of bliss with her modern Adam. Knowledge of Harry's temptation by Pearl, and his fall, means the end of Bertha's fantasy-heaven, her expulsion from the symbolic garden. Mansfield has quite clearly prepared for her protagonist's realization that all is not well by the earlier scene in which Bertha shudders upon seeing one cat chasing another in her garden. "What creepy things cats are" (p. 341) points ahead to the unwholesome alliance between Pearl and Bertha's husband.

Had Katherine Mansfield been willing to settle for this relatively uncomplicated symbolic intrusion, explication of the story might suitably end here. But "Bliss" represents one of the few attempts by this writer to be cerebral in the artificial, contrived sense of the word—cerebral in the way she criticized in other writers.[3] The outcome is a heavy weight of analogies and correspondences whose import is questionable and whose value is doubtful.

In an apparent attempt to universalize the meaning of her story, Mansfield attires her heroine in the garb of a pear tree and allows "her petals" to rustle "softly into the hall" (p. 342). At the same time, Pearl Fulton is elaborately presented as no less a figure than the moon itself. Silverhaired Pearl (note the name) always carries her head a little to one side. She is cool and comes out at night. She has "moonbeam fingers" and eventually she seeks the garden where she and Bertha experience their deepest communion.

> And the two women stood side by side looking at the slender, flowering tree. Although it was so still it seemed, like the flame of a candle, to stretch up, to point, to quiver in the bright air, to grow taller and taller as they gazed—almost to touch the rim of the round, silver moon.
>
> How long did they stand there? Both, as it were, caught in that circle of unearthly light, understanding each other perfectly, creatures of another world, and wondering what they were to do in this one with all this blissful treasure that burned in their bosoms and dropped, in silver flowers, from their hair and hands? (p. 347)

Utter bliss seems possible, then, for creatures of another world. Moons and trees may communicate their blissful state without words: "And did Miss Fulton murmur: 'Yes, Just *that.*' Or did Bertha dream it?" (p. 347).

Yet identification of Pearl with moon and Bertha with tree raises a great many questions of Mansfield's intent. For Bertha is a pear tree all right, but there is also no question that the tree, in the scene quoted above, is a very phallic symbol that attracts, almost mesmerizes, the two women in the garden. As such, it ought to be identifiable with Harry, who divides his attentions and his masculinity between the two. Such a reading would have the pear tree act as symbolic representation of both Harry and his wife, in two very different ways—an unusual and confusing use of symbol, to say the least.

There is considerable evidence, however, that this is precisely what Katherine Mansfield intends. Moreover, the entire story seems to be constructed around the notion of doubles, of other selves. The author had used the device before and in a quite obvious way, notably with Beryl in "Prelude," who, as she writes a letter to her friend, reflects that there is within her another self that the recipient of the letter will never know, a self utterly different from and at odds with the cheerful, young thing the letter presents.[4] Mansfield herself comments in one of her letters that she senses the presence of "a second you who is outside yourself and does nothing . . . and then there is this keen, unsleeping creature—waiting to leap." In another letter to her husband, previously quoted, she had underlined the necessity not to "lower your mask until you have another mask prepared beneath—as terrible as you like—but a mask."[5]

In "Bliss," all the characters seem to wear at least one mask, to have at least one other self. Mansfield develops this motif most obviously in her depiction of the Norman Knights where, even in her choice of the name, she suggests the difficulty of distinguishing one Knight from the other. Further, they have given each other the nicknames "Face" and "Mug" to reinforce the idea of indistinguishability. Their conversational idiom demonstrates as well their extreme likeness: "The cream of it was when she, being full fed, turned to the woman beside her and said: 'Haven't you ever seen a monkey before?' " "Oh, yes!" Mrs. Norman Knight joined in the laughter. "Wasn't that too absolutely creamy?" (pp. 342–43). To make sure that her point is clear, Mansfield associates this couple with a "monkey" motif. Mrs. Knight has monkeys on her coat and she herself looks like "a very intelligent monkey" (p. 343). The idea of imitation and of mimicking is firmly established. The dividing line between men and women has become blurred in the society which Mansfield describes. The emancipated woman has lost possession of her child to the hired nurse. Both Norman Knights work in the world of illusion, the husband in the theater, the wife as interior decorator.

Beyond this social commentary, moreover, Mansfield seems to be getting at the point that human relationships are unsatisfactory in the world she knew and that, more significant, the individual himself is fragmented into pitifully inadequate segments of personality. "Bliss" seems to be the story of the attempt of various disparate segments to establish relationships with other segments—and the inevitable failure to do so meaningfully.

Thus, the notion of the pear tree as both Harry and Bertha becomes tenable. In its phallic sense (for Harry is Mansfield's stereotype of the loud, self-assured, aggressive male on a hunt for sexual satisfaction), the tree represents the passionate fulfillment both women now covet from the male. As "the lovely pear tree with its wide open blossoms" that Bertha sees "as a symbol of her own life" (p. 342), it is a measure of how far reality falls short of Bertha's dream of the future.

Katherine Mansfield sets up, as complement to the Norman Knight pair and the Young couple, a series of interlocking segmented relationships. Thus, Eddie Warren and Harry appear to be drawn as a polarity whose merging would form a well-balanced person. Effeminate Eddie, with his affected, ladylike speech is balanced by masculine Harry, with his manly voice and power over women. Eddie is frightened of a dream while Harry has a passion for fighting. Though we find at the end of the story that Pearl Fulton is Harry's "moon," the reader is told earlier that the pear tree would be "silver now, in the light of poor dear Eddie's moon, silver as Miss Fulton" (p. 346). So Miss Fulton is the property of Eddie as much as of Harry in this strange combination.

Pearl and Bertha also form an interesting pair of opposites whose paths converge. Bertha, the mature, blooming wife has heretofore lived a platonic married life with Harry. She has felt herself to be cold and, ultimately, unfulfilled though she has every reason and opportunity for fulfillment. Pearl, on the other hand, as the moon, stands for chastity, coldness, distance and unapproachability—"green and cold," reminding Harry of the "green of pistachio ices." Yet it is Pearl who is involved in a passionate relationship with Harry. The added complication is that Bertha appears to find almost sexual excitement—certainly emotional fulfillment—in contact not with her husband but with her husband's paramour, Miss Fulton. She is Bertha's "find." [6] Bliss is attainable only in her presence and her touch. And at the pear tree, both women, the cold and the warm, the married and the spinster, the sleepy and the exhilarated, the loved and the unloved, find communion in sharing. The thing shared, however, turns out to be Harry as tree, and the experience is satisfactory only when the two women, disparate segments finally in communion, stand together.

The idea that the Norman Knights have one personality between them, that Eddie and Harry are representative of the poles of masculinity, that Pearl and Bertha somehow embody between them the contradiction and the promise of womanhood is perhaps strengthened by the manner in which Katherine Mansfield refers to the two cats in the garden: "A grey cat, dragging its belly, crept across the lawn, and a black one, *its shadow,* [italics mine] trailed after" (p. 341). From the language, it is impossible to know precisely whether the author is speaking of one cat or more with respect to this motif of doubles. Toward the end of the story, as the guests are leaving for the night, Eddie first glides "noiselessly" after Bertha, and then, on the same page, Miss Fulton leaves "with Eddie following, like the black cat following the grey cat" (p. 350). It will be noted that Eddie follows both women (doubles) indiscriminately in the first instance; and that in pursuing Pearl, in the second instance, he assumes the role of his opposite, Harry, whose tomcat activities with Miss Fulton have sullied the purity of the garden.

Katherine Mansfield does not stop with a description of these divided people as psychological cases. The whole party, rather, is treated as broad social satire, comic, though as with Bertha's epiphany, fraught with pain. Mansfield knew the social set she described as well as she was to know any group of English people in the early years of the century. "*Eddie* of course is a fish out of the ______ pond," she confided to her husband in a letter dated February 28, 1918. "And Harry is touched with W. L. G[eorge]." "Miss Fulton," she added, "is my own invention." [7] Bringing the entire perverse, unwholesome, shallow group together at a dinner party, she is able like Chekhov to demonstrate through their interaction—and even more so through their inability often to interact—the essential deadness of the ostensibly lively party group.

Like Joyce in "The Dead," Katherine Mansfield deals in great detail with food, but whereas the Irish writer restricted his treatment to a scrupulous description of the festal board, Mansfield employs food imagery throughout the story, even where it has apparently nothing to do with the contents of the meal. The arrangement of the fruit in its bowl is given in detail. Little B. is glimpsed at her solitary meal. The Norman Knights find the situation on the train "too asbolutely creamy," and Mrs. Knight's dress seems to have been made from banana skins, her earrings "like little dangling nuts" (p. 343). "Michael *Oat*" (italics mine) has written a play which one guest suggests may be called "Stomach Trouble" (p. 345). Harry glories in "the white flesh of the lobster" and the "green of pistachio ices" (p. 345). Bilks has a new poem called "Table d'Hôte," in which the first line is "Why Must it Always be Tomato Soup?" (p. 349).

This concentration upon the digestive process and the raw materials of ingestion and digestion in a story entitled "Bliss" suggests the ironic revulsion Mansfield apparently feels toward the world she describes. Since the main stock in trade of its denizens it talk, the mouth becomes the principal weapon of the circle. And when the mouths are not full of words, they are full of food. The grossness and materiality of such a society, behind the brittle facade of bohemianism and spirituality, calls for imagery that will stress the physical, almost the animal, in the participants. Thus, the cats in the garden become a fitting submotif to accompany the motif of food.[8]

Though not strictly relevant to an explication of this story, it is interesting that Mansfield herself is often described by writers of memoirs as the only silent one among talkative artists at one gathering after another.[9] Sitting buddhalike, with enormous composure, taking everything in, she maintained the distance and reserve that set her apart from the others. To the extent that one concentrates on this aspect of Mansfield's attitudes, she can in no way be identified with Bertha, a rather silly woman carried away by her closeness to the modern, flippant, avant garde generation.

One other subsidiary motif commends itself for at least cursory treatment. Eddie Warren introduces the idea of "*driving* through Eternity in a *timeless* taxi" (p. 343) when, upon arrival, he describes the trip to Bertha's residence. The "sinister" cab driver had refused to stop for him to alight and had carried him on faster and faster. Perhaps the story is told merely to show in a few words Eddie's high-strung nature and his effeminate way of talking. But the Norman Knights also stress the events of their train journey to the dinner party, emphasizing how they themselves were completely at odds with all the other middle-class passengers. Later on, upon departure from the party, Mrs. Knight confesses herself and her husband to be "victims of time and train" (p. 348). Finally, Miss Fulton offers to let Eddie "come part of the way in my taxi" (p. 349).

In this treatment by Katherine Mansfield of London's bohemian wasteland, both "straight" and ironic association with Marvell's coy mistress are germane. The story is full of mistresses: not only Pearl Fulton but "the weirdest little person" who is "very *liée* with Michael Oat" (p. 345), and, whimsically, the cat being wooed in Bertha's garden. These modern creatures are courted in a specially ugly, unwholesome, almost perverse manner by swains not nearly as frank and outspoken as Marvell's lover. As in Eliot's *Prufrock* and *The Waste Land*, or Waugh's *A Handful of Dust* (where the level of society examined more nearly approximates Mansfield's people), contrast with the past through associative devices accentuates the meanness of the present.

Beyond this facet of the association, Mansfield's concentration on that part of the poem which deals with the encroaching power of time, the advent of old age and death, and the sound of time's winged chariot (now become a taxi whose driver refuses to stop for the passenger; or a train whose occupants disapprove of nonconformist riders) enriches her story of Bertha *Young*. For Bertha's hope to sustain her state of bliss, to keep the pear tree always in the full bloom of perfect maturity, with no undeveloped buds and no fading petals, is blasted in advance by Marvell's chill observations on time and eternity.

In addition, though Mansfield in her criticism ordinarily is scornful of writers who attempt to introduce Freudian concepts or even Freudian symbols into their fiction, in "Bliss" she appears to be doing just that. Eddie's taxi driver has a "*flattened* head" (p. 343) (Mansfield's italics). Michael Oat's weird little creature has cut off her hair and has "taken a dreadfully good snip off her legs and arms and her neck and her poor little nose as well" (p. 345). And Eddie Warren speaks of a poem about "a *girl* who was *violated* by a beggar *without* a nose in a lit-tle wood" (p. 347). The whole tenor of these seemingly gratuitous descriptions of characters who do not play a direct part in the story is sickly, unwholesome, and sexually degrading. To cut off one's hair is to surrender one's sexual power. The two missing noses are suggestive of a castration motif, or at least of emasculation and sexual weakness. In a story of contemporary Prufrocks, of Bertha and Pearl, of Eddie Warren and the Knights, a girl's violation by an emasculated beggar is much more likely than the amorous conquest of the "Lady" by her lusty suitor in the Marvell poem.

"Bliss" is an excellent example of a story and a protagonist suggested to its author by one of her own moods —and yet not an autobiographical story in its finished form. To Lady Ottoline Morrell Mansfield had written in 1919:

O this Spring—It makes me long for happiness. That is so vague. Each year I think—this year I shall not feel it so keenly—but I feel it more. Why are human beings the only ones who do not put forth fresh buds—exquisite flowers and leaves? I cannot bear to go among them. I sit here or take small walks and there seems a blessing fallen upon the world just as long as one does not see the people or know of their ways. . . . Really, on some of these days one is tired with *bliss* [Mansfield's italics]. I long to tell someone—to feel it immediately shared—felt without my asking "do you feel it?"—Do you know what I mean? [10]

All the elements of "Bliss" are here, even the title, yet Mansfield has withdrawn from the center, particularized the point of view to Bertha, introduced the social satire, regulated the imagery strictly so that it conveys something different from, and much more than, the sentimental passage in the letter. Though Mansfield was not entirely satisfied with the story, her control of all the elements within it puts it clearly among the masterful creations of her last four years.

"Marriage à la Mode" is in the tradition of "Bliss," both stories in which a domestic tragedy is played out against a backround of broad social satire. In both instances, the flamboyant, articulate, utterly silly pseudo-bohemian set is the target of Mansfield's scorn though in the former story they play a greater role in the personal catastrophe than in the latter. Both Bertha Young and her husband, though they enjoy the company of people like Eddie Warren and the Norman Knights, maintain a distance from the circle—observers rather than participants. And the character who brings down their flimsy marital structure, Pearl Fulton, is instantly recognizable as another outsider. In "Marriage," it is precisely that the husband cannot be seduced into the bohemian circle while his wife Isabel is charmed away from reality by its members which produces the rupture. Though Isabel has a momentary epiphany of a sort before the charm takes hold again, it is the husband's turn, in this story, to recognize the impossibility of life with his wife so long as she is unable to free herself from its pernicious influence.

The author makes clear that, to William at least, life

before the advent of the bohemians had been idyllic. Even in urban London, he had been able to grow petunias and to revel in the innocent joy of his young love for Isabel—for him similar in retrospect to the sublime experience of the boy in "Something Childish But Very Natural." William is particularly drawn to the world of childhood in his revulsion from the perverse adult world of his wife's pals. As he looks out of the train window, what attracts him is "a wide river, with naked children splashing in the shallows" (p. 556). His thoughts on the train are of his own children and the gifts he would bring to them. Though it is painful to think of his grown-up Isabel, he can remember with pleasure his wife on vacation in the old days, wearing " a jersey and her hair in a plait; she looked about fourteen" (p. 558). Even he himself, in reverie, is "still that little boy" (p. 556) who used to shake the rain-soaked rosebush over himself.

This freshness and natural beauty of childhood acts as a sustaining force in William's life when he is unable to bear the present state of his marital affairs. He will not bring anything mechanical or sophisticated to his children; rather he chooses a pineapple and a melon, the delights of nature, to please them. His worry is that even this simple gift may be diverted to the bohemians who surround his wife. "Isabel's friends could hardly go sneaking up to the nursery at the children's mealtimes. All the same, as he bought the melon William had a horrible vision of one of Isabel's young poets lapping up a slice . . . behind the nursery door" (p. 555).

By nightmare juxtapositions of this kind, Mansfield balances the fresh beauty of childhood and nature with another view of childhood, ugly and grotesquely perverse. "Be nice to him, my children" (p. 560), says Isabel *not* to Paddy and Johnny but to her bohemian circle. And the group is, without doubt, painted as a pack of horrible children whose freshness is utterly missing and whose relationship to nature is hardly pastoral. William has good reason to worry that the fruit intended for his little ones will be diverted by the clownish, insatiable adults. Moira Morrison's bonnet is "like a hugh strawberry" (p. 558), a perversion of nature, and she "jumped up and down" (p. 558) like a youngster. The effeminate Bobby Kane buys children's candy from a shop and, childlike, forgets to pay for it. Bill Hunt, like a perverse, overly imaginative child, imagines that the packages containing the fruits really conceal "de-cap-it-ated heads!" (p. 559). These are people playing at being children and failing to carry off the pretense. Their encounter with nature at the water (so different from the view of the naked children bathing that William sees from the train window) is capped by their visit to a pub for "sloe gin."

As she does in "Bliss," Mansfield makes full use of the imagery, and perhaps the symbolism, of food. Usurpers not only of William's hearth and his wife, the bohemian crew figuratively eats William out of house and home. Even the title of the story hints at the motif of eating. The displacement of one set of children by the other is dramatized by the fate of the love offering William brings to his family—the pineapple and melon rejected for his own offspring by Isabel and turned over by her to the outsiders.

Imagery of food abounds, from the sweets of Bobby Kane to the fish which the group must accept if it wishes to have ice. They speak of anointing themselves with butter. They dine on sardines and whiskey. And even when the talk turns to the color of one's legs under water, Moira describes hers as of "the palest, palest mushroom colour" (p. 561). All eat "enormously" except, apparently, William, the "stranger" to the group and, now, to his own wife. Within him, instead, there is a "dull, persistent gnawing" (p. 556), now grown "familiar," which abates only when William is able to get his mind off his marriage. This gnawing sensation, though not attributed to a specific bodily source in the story, seems clearly to be a pang of psychological hunger. His marital situation allows for no nourishment either for the children or for himself. Isabel has turned her attention elsewhere. His choice of the fruits as gifts had been his way, unconsciously, of offering at least to the deprived children (and he is, as has been noted, one of them) the nourishment of love, but even these had gone to fatten the usurpers of his contentment.

Freudian implications aside, Mansfield's concentration on the imagery of food and eating represents an appropriate rendering of the "vile, odious, abominable, vulgar" (p. 564) presence of grossness in the band of usurpers: a grossness now beginning to rub off on Isabel. As in "Bliss," all the pseudo-sophisticated small talk of the ballet, of aesthetic considerations, and the like cannot hide the elemental coarseness of the bohemians. Their role as destructive parasites is thoroughly established. As a consequence, they are stamped with the parasite's symbolic mark and made voracious eaters of the substance of another creature. Indeed, the reference to the "mushroom" quality of Moira's legs under water is less obscure when one realizes that the mushroom is a parasitic fungus. No less interesting in this regard is Bobby Kane's last name, reminiscent of another Cain who lived at the expense of his brother.

A Midsummer Night's Dream is invoked too in the story through Moira's habit of calling Isabel "Titania." That Isabel should be queen of the fairies is doubly meaningful in "Marriage à la Mode." That she should be estranged from her husband also fits the pattern. Most significant is the bewitching of Titania in Shakespeare's play so that the exquisite queen finds Bottom a handsome and desirable companion. She cannot see the ass's head as gross and grotesque nor does she recognize how far she has fallen from her usual high standards. Bewitched, Titania offers the absurd Bottom "what thou desirest to eat," and Bottom, half man, half animal (like the bohemians) chooses to "munch your good dry oats." Ironically for the modern couple, William is no Oberon nor is the idea of bewitching Isabel his. It is left for the less noble and exalted William to deplore the charm that has been placed upon Isabel but to be unable except for a brief moment to break the spell. The modern Titania never entirely wakes from the dream and her husband, therefore, must seek to escape the nightmare through renunciation and flight.

Meaningfully, in the picture of midsummer that Mansfield offers, both protagonists live in dream: William seeking relief in the fantasy of his childhood past and his married life before the descent of the bohemians; Isabel in the nightmare spell itself cast by her companions. There is evidence, however, that the wife has invited her bewitched state—that she had never been truly content with the idyll of normal marriage and motherhood. Perhaps the reader is to see the bohemian clan as merely the expression of Isabel's inner state, dramatized for fictional presentation. As Bertha Young in "Bliss" finds in Pearl Fulton both a nemesis and a secret sharer, so in this story Moira Morrison may function both as enchantress and as the expression of Isabel's deepest nature, evoking in the wife what Isabel most wishes to have evoked. Perhaps the presence of both elements in Isabel explains the painting that William sees in the sitting room:

> On the wall opposite William some one had painted a young man, over lifesize, with very wobbly legs, offering a wide-eyed daisy to a young woman who had one very short arm and one very long, thin one. (p. 560)

William's simple, natural offer of love is made to a woman whose aspect is distorted and grotesque—a combination of two persons of varying appearance. The auguries for a successful marriage are not auspicious.

In one of her most memorable stories, Mansfield returns to domestic tragedy again. Her critical sense told her justly that in "The Daughters of the Late Colonel" she had written a remarkable story. "A huge long story of a rather new kind," she called it, "the outcome of the *Prelude* method—it just unfolds and opens." At its completion near the end of 1920, she felt her increasing mastery, and could report confidently to Richard Murry that "the technique is stronger" here than in "The Prelude." [11]

Her sympathy with human nature demonstrates her maturity as a person, a maturity very likely deepened by her own desperate situation. Realization on her part of her ability to examine character with heightened sensitivity made it particularly difficult to accept misunderstanding of what she had tried to do:

> I confess I hoped very much that my readers would understand what I was trying to express. But very few did. They thought it was "cruel"; they thought I was "sneering" at Jug and Constantia; or they thought it was "drab." And in the last paragraph I was "poking fun at the poor old things." [12]

Actually, what confused such readers was the skill of the author in suggesting facets of personality rather than depending on explicit statement. Also, Mansfield's manipulation of point of view, her artful juggling of the time sequence, and her technique of eliminating the distinction among levels of reality, while they improved the story, discouraged the readers.

"The Daughters of the Late Colonel" is deliberately constructed on a foundation of vagueness and indecisiveness. That the father of Josephine and Constantia

had been a colonel, a military man who lived his life in a strict, disciplined, patterned, decisive way, is no accident. By terrorizing his children into unthinking obedience, he had effectively rendered them helpless at his death to reverse the pattern. It is much easier to be cajoled by Cyril or browbeaten by Kate or overawed by Miss Andrews than to assert their supremacy in their own household. Deference to the needs of others in small things had over the years meant deference in the major areas of existence—love, marriage, withdrawal, subserviency to paternal tyranny, the inability of self-assertion and, worse, the inability to know even the terms on which self-assertion is called for. As the title suggests, the sisters had given up an independent existence, surrendered any other relationship save the one as "daughters" to a "colonel," and therefore found themselves at his death rudderless, leaderless, and drifting.

It is this latter quality of drifting that Mansfield seeks in every way to express and to exemplify through the story. In the frighteningly hazy and directionless world of Constantia and Josephine, time has no meaning and no boundaries. The present is no more real than the past or the future. Life and death have no fixed limits, and therefore the dead father is seen as just as much alive as before his heart stopped beating. Even the inanimate world of wardrobes and chests is invested with animate characteristics and looms menacingly at the two fearful "tabbies." Sun and moon, finally, become mysteriously involved with these earth creatures as the vague dialogue at the end discloses the inevitability of lives that have drifted too long for salvage.

Mansfield's prose technique is quite up to the task of rendering the vagueness: "The week after was one of the busiest. . . . their minds went on, thinking things out . . . trying to remember where . . . [final ellipsis Mansfield's]" (p. 463). The reader does not know until later what the "after" refers to and never does find out what the "where" signifies. Nor at the end of the story, when Constantia has "something frightfully important" (p. 483) to say to her sister, does she ever get to express it "because I've forgotten what it was . . . that I was going to say" (p. 483). As she says this, she turns "with one of her vague gestures." Between the two examples here cited, the story sets up and maintains this rhythm of querulous indecisiveness.

The fact that the sisters live in this hazy never-never land where Time like a drunkard weaves back and forth allows Mansfield thematic justification for her liberties with chronology in writing the story. Like Faulkner's Miss Emily,[13] whose notion of time is vague and who confuses her dead father with the live father she once had, her dead lover with the Homer Barron who once wooed her, the sisters cannot exist in the definite realm of clock time, for, given their present state, such an existence would be insupportable. They must be able to shift from the present into the more comfortable time of the past or the fantasy life of the future in order for the "now" to be at all possible. Josephine's big worry is thus what father would "say when he found out" (p. 469) that the girls had had him buried and that he would never forgive them for their role in his interment.

Mansfield's manipulation of time in the story is best seen in her treatment of Cyril's visit. Josephine decides that the colonel's grandson Cyril ought to inherit the old man's watch. (It might be noted that the author makes a point of its being a timepiece rather than cuff-links or fountain pen). She projects forward in time and imagines a future visit by Cyril during which she will comment on the fact that he is wearing his grandfather's watch. This train leads her to remember the recent past when Cyril had apologized by mail for his inability to attend the funeral. From this thought, she switches to the future, when the boy has promised to stop by for tea; and to memories of times in the past when he has come to tea. At this point, without introduction of any kind, Mansfield presents a teatime conversation involving Cyril and his two aunts. It is deliberately impossible to tell at first whether it is a record of what has occurred in the past, or whether it is an exposition of an actual new tea party, or whether Josephine is fantasizing, imagining what their future tea party will be like. Two pages later, Mansfield reveals that at the party in question "Father" was still alive, so the event is fixed in the past. Until that point, however, the reader is forced to experience the same vagueness with regard to time that the sisters feel—with a corresponding comprehension of their cobwebby manner of grappling with reality.

During the tea party conversation (pp. 475–76) much is made of time by the participants, as Mansfield plays variations on her theme. Cyril has to justify his lack of appetite by citing the lateness of his lunch. Josephine responds that it is "after four" now. The question of whether his father liked meringues is put off by Cyril with the excuse that "it's such a long time since—" and he pleads the lateness of the hour as his excuse for leaving: "I say, Auntie Con, isn't your clock a bit slow?" Ironically and meaningfully, Constantia "couldn't make up her mind if it was fast or slow," but is sure that it is "one or the other." Then, after a section in which Cyril is taken into the presence of the colonel, Josephine returns to the present, saying:

> "Yes, I shall send Cyril the watch. . . ."
>
> "That would be very nice," said Constantia. "I seem to remember last time he came there was some little trouble about the time."

This overwhelming concern with time in the Cyril episode, when reinforced by the earlier passages in which the two sisters imagine their father's watch being delivered to Benny in the jungle, confirms the importance that the author placed on this element as a motif and as a structural device. It is summed up in Constantia's thoughts about the clock—"one or the other," either "fast or slow." This is the story of her life and of her sister's.

Though confined to a much smaller space in the narrative, the motif of sun and moon appears equally significant. Writing in her *Journal*, Mansfield confesses to a deep interest in cosmic anatomy: "What attracts me . . . it's that reactions to certain causes and effects always have been the same. It wasn't for nothing Constantia chose the moon and water, for instance." [14] Mansfield saves the motif for the twelfth and final section of the story when the organ-grinder's music recalls to the sisters that their father is really dead and won't complain about the noise. At this moment, the sun appears on the carpet and slowly spreads its rays about the room till it lights up their dead mother's photograph.

Imagery of the sun as a potentially warming and liberating force is not new in contemporary literature. Ibsen had used it more than once, and Joyce, in the first story of *Dubliners*,[15] has the protagonist walk in the sunshine and feel a sense of freedom after he knows for certain that Father Flynn is dead. Here too in

"The Daughters of the Late Colonel," realization of the father's death is the signal for the appearance of the sun. Its presence may also be explained in terms of the epiphany concerning their own lives which the sisters almost achieve, the illumination of their darkness. For Constantia, the presence of the sun is coupled with her hope of a definite message from her inscrutable Buddha figure on the mantelpiece. Like her, this Buddha has seemed always less than definite—smiling noncommittally. Now, as the sun "thieved" its way into the room, the Buddha seems on the verge of a revelation and Constantia, in a new attitude, stood before it, but "not as usual, not vaguely" (p. 482).

Yet, it is of the moon she wonders, not the sun, and of her youth. She had crept "out of her bed in her nightgown when the moon was full, and lain on the floor with her arms outstretched, as though she was crucified. Why? The big, pale moon had made her do it" (p. 482). She recalls too how, as a youngster, she had tried to get as close to the sea as possible to gaze at the "restless water" (p. 483). The ordinary events in her life, she concludes, were unreal; her real self was expressed only in the moonlight or by the sea.

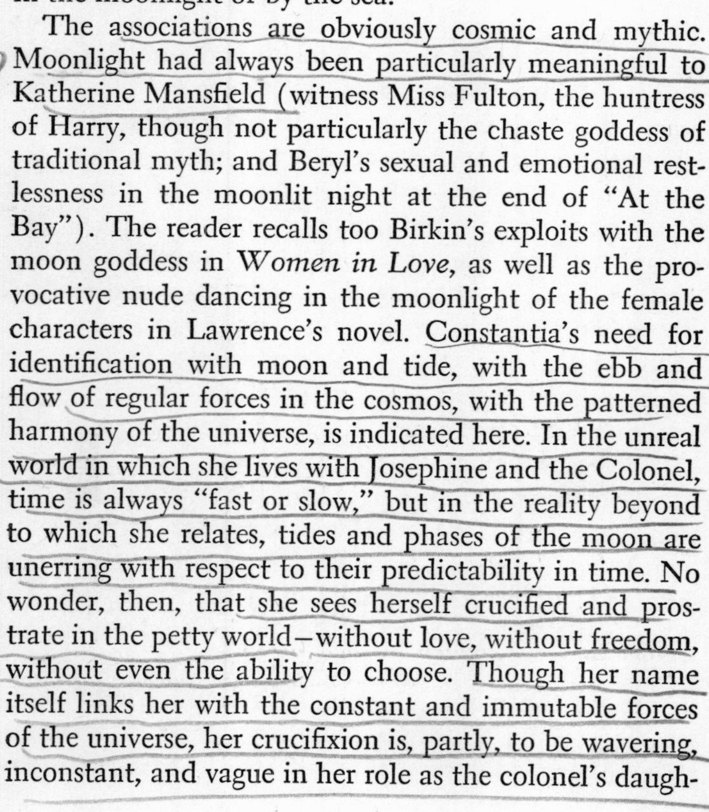

The associations are obviously cosmic and mythic. Moonlight had always been particularly meaningful to Katherine Mansfield (witness Miss Fulton, the huntress of Harry, though not particularly the chaste goddess of traditional myth; and Beryl's sexual and emotional restlessness in the moonlit night at the end of "At the Bay"). The reader recalls too Birkin's exploits with the moon goddess in *Women in Love*, as well as the provocative nude dancing in the moonlight of the female characters in Lawrence's novel. Constantia's need for identification with moon and tide, with the ebb and flow of regular forces in the cosmos, with the patterned harmony of the universe, is indicated here. In the unreal world in which she lives with Josephine and the Colonel, time is always "fast or slow," but in the reality beyond to which she relates, tides and phases of the moon are unerring with respect to their predictability in time. No wonder, then, that she sees herself crucified and prostrate in the petty world—without love, without freedom, without even the ability to choose. Though her name itself links her with the constant and immutable forces of the universe, her crucifixion is, partly, to be wavering, inconstant, and vague in her role as the colonel's daugh-

ter. Finally, in the sense that the moon has sexual implications as, in Jung's view, the sea does too, Constantia's crucifixion is a sexual one, and what it was "she was always wanting" is not hard to guess (p. 483).

The sun playing its rays on the photograph of their mother evokes from the more practical and logical Josephine thoughts of childhood, of the difference the postponed death of their mother might have made in their lives, and of the possibilities of love and marriage for herself and her sister when they were young. Though less dramatic than her sister's epiphany, the knowledge that the crying sound she hears comes not from the sparrows but from within herself is equally terrifying. While Constantia does not know why she experiences an affinity for sea and moon, Josephine deliberates upon her own single state and shows that she understands what the cry is about. Ruminating, she is touched by the sun and lifting her face to it, "she was drawn over to the window by gentle beams" (p. 482). Like Laura in "The Garden Party," who feels the flowers growing within her, like Bertha, the pear tree of "Bliss," Josephine becomes a flower momentarily warmed by the sun—but only momentarily. "She stared at a big cloud where the sun had been" (p. 483). Constantia may identify with sea and moon; for her sister, it is sun and flower. But both briefly inhabit what is for them the ultimate world of heightened reality. In a letter to William Gerhardi, who admired the story, Mansfield had written in 1921:

> There was a moment when I first had the "idea" when I saw the two sisters as *amusing;* but . . . I bowed down to the beauty that was hidden in their lives and to discover that was all my desire. . . . All was meant . . . to lead up to that last paragraph when my two flowerless ones turned . . . to the sun. . . . And after that . . . they died as surely as Father was dead.[16]

Constantia's predilection for the moon and the sea and Josephine's for the sun point obliquely to one of Mansfield's emerging strengths in this story and some that follow. With some justice, critics have noted that she deals in her early work with a narrow range of characters, and that, even within that range, stereotypes of characterization are frequent. The pseudo-sophisticated upper-class wife, the servant girl preyed upon by brutal men, the young couple learning about life from daily exposure to small problems—these and other people in her stories seem often, except for superficial differences, indistinguishable. The complaint is that, living her life of semi-invalidism in hotel after hotel at a distance from the other guests and deprived of close emotional involvement with other human beings except through correspondence, Mansfield never got close enough to learn about individual differences or discriminating enough to delineate them.

In "The Daughters of the Late Colonel," however, Mansfield turns what might have become stock description of two doddering, insecure old maids into two quite separate pictures of individuals. From the opening dialogue between the sisters, and with almost no peripheral interference from the author, Josephine is established as the more venturesome and aggressive of the two. Her tongue is sharper, her sense of humor more evident. Even thinking of her dead father and his bowler hat, she can giggle at a random thought. She is practical where Constantia is not, and sees no objection to putting off mourning at home since "nobody sees us" (p. 464). She snaps at her sister. She can be "furious." It is unnecessary to detail further the way in which Mansfield sets up the differences between the daughters, culminating in the sun and moon affinities at the end. Though she needs considerably fewer pages than Arnold Bennett uses in his *Old Wives' Tale* to distinguish his heroines, the task is just as thoroughly accomplished.

This story is also a good example of its author's employment of multiple point of view. Apparently unbothered by the fashion of the new century or by Henry James's strictures on fiction, Mansfield allows—even encourages—the point of view to shift from one character to another and sometimes from character to narrator. The first paragraph presents a point of view common to both sisters. Then, in the ensuing dialogue, though the reader is mainly in the mind of Josephine, at one point when Constantia thinks of hungry mice not finding a crumb in their home, the reader learns that "She wished she'd left a tiny piece of biscuit on the dressing table. It was awful to think of it not finding anything. What would it do?" (p. 465). But a few lines further on, when the annoyed Josephine accuses her sister of being asleep and therefore of talking foolishness, the story reads: " ' I don't think I am,' said Constantia. She shut her eyes to make sure. She was." Until the last two words, the reader is back in Constantia's orbit. The archness of "She was," however, can hardly be Constantia's. If it is Mansfield's narrator who takes over here, the uncalled-for cuteness of the line is jarring to the basic seriousness of the fiction, and represents a throwback to the Mansfield of the *German Pension* tales.

"The Stranger," completed in November 1920, is probably Mansfield's most compelling study in loneliness—her own and the archetypal loneliness that besets the human animal. Piqued by what she took to be Murry's slight of this story when she mailed it to him for comment and disposition, she exclaims in a letter dated November 17, 1920: "Richard [Murry] will draw posters 100 years. Praise him when I'm dead. Talk to ME. I'm lonely. I haven't ONE single soul." [17] But the story is not personal and the loneliness involved is universal, frighteningly limitless, and pervasive for both the living and the dead.

Its universality, perhaps, is what impels so many commentators to find in it parallels to James Joyce's "The Dead," in which Gabriel Conroy's successive retreats from private involvement at the annual party of his aunts culminate in the discovery that he will never again find total fulfillment with his own wife after the knowledge that a young man, now dead, had once been in love with her. What begins as Gabriel's personal psychological problem, becomes before the end of the story the tragedy of all Dubliners and, by extension, the plight of all men in the contemporary world. Though Mansfield chooses to end "The Stranger" at the moment of Mr. Hammond's epiphany—his realization that he will never truly be alone with Janey again—the ripples of implication throughout the story suggest the wider interpretation.

As in the Joyce story, Mansfield relies a great deal on irony for her effects. "The Stranger" mentioned in the title turns out to be not the dying man on board the ship who dies in Janey's arms but Janey to her husband. The most intimate relationship among adults is reduced to a contractual bargain: whenever Mr. Hammond kisses his wife, Janey's response merely "signed the contract" (p. 456). The hints are numerous that the marriage relationship had always been one of distance and duty for the wife, even before the long separation geographically occurred. The further irony is that Janey had seemed much closer to her husband when he was forced to fantasize about their connection in her absence than she seems when he holds her in his arms. The ultimate horror is that the unnamed dead man—a shade, a memory—will forever come between the two as Michael Furey destroys Gabriel Conroy's relationship, however imperfect, with Gretta.

Mansfield knows precisely what she wants to do at the outset of the story to prepare the way for the epiphany of the husband at the end. Elsewhere in this book, her involvement with the place and the people of the story has been described. The imagery in which she clothes the description of the distant ship in the harbor is unpleasantly revelatory of the physical aspect of Hammond's needs. The water is a "grey crinkled tablecloth" (p. 446); the deck is the dish on that cloth. Just as the gulls dive for "the galley droppings at the stern" (p. 446), the passengers, from this distance, are "little flies walking up and down the dish," strolling in "couples" and presumably taking their nourishment from the leavings on the plate. One of the crewmen is seen as "a tiny black spider" (p. 446). In the context of Mansfield's work, these images suggest physical desire, the satisfaction of bodily lusts, the vaguely outlined sin of animal gluttony.

By way of contrast, Mansfield presents Mr. Hammond as the acme of restraint, good taste, and measured propriety—at least to outward appearances: gloves, overcoat, scarf, hat, and folded umbrella. "Something between the sheep-dog and the shepherd" (p. 446), he "roped in" with his glance the rest of the crowd. His clothing and manner are true indices of his personality. A self-centered man, he ascribes to others the same attitudes as he possesses. He can be arrogant except where his wife is concerned. He is compulsive in his neatness and in the precision with which he keeps track of the time. That his watch is "butter-yellow" (p. 447), however, shows the futility of trying to account for each moment. Like butter, time melts in the subjective sense, and shortly Hammond will be eternally living in the time of the night before, when his wife held the stranger in her arms.

Hammond's treatment of the little girl at the wharf is obviously meaningful too. "Little" Jean Scott's plaintive cry for her afternoon tea reminds him that, perhaps, on deck his wife Janey may be taking tea and allows him to imagine himself a hero making the desired beverage materialize for her. "And for a moment he was on deck, standing over her, watching her little hand fold round the cup" (pp. 447–48). As the little girl continues to cry, he swings her to a higher barrel. "The movement of holding her, steadying her, relieved him wonderfully, lightened his heart" (p. 448). But when the boat begins to move in toward shore, the solicitious Hammond "had forgotten about Jean. He sprang away to greet old Captain Johnson" (p. 448).

The reader will note the similarity between the names of Jane and Jean, the small child being, in effect, a temporary substitute for Hammond's wife. What Hammond does for Jean is, in a sense, to act out the role of hero and protector that his fantasy has just evoked. Not truly interested in the child for herself, he abandons her as soon as her counterpart on the boat begins to move in his direction. Even in the moment of closeness to Jean, *he* is shown to be the dependent one who draws from the contact a certain measure of relief and a lightened heart. Furthermore, Mansfield takes pains to show that "*little* Jean Scott" is a childhood version of small Janey. The word "little" and its synonyms are used over and over to call attention to the parallel. Jean is "the little girl," a "poor little beggar," and a "little pal of mine"; while Janey has a "little voice," a "small hand," and writes baggage labels in "her little clear hand." He finds her, after a ten-month absence, "just her little self." It would seem incontrovertable from this evidence that Mansfield intends Hammond's encounter with Jean to foreshadow his traumatic conversation with his wife. In its revelation of his motivations, the earlier incident also explains to some degree the real or imagined coldness that Hammond senses in Janey. If this little piece of wifely property has been hitherto used in the same way as Jean—to give Hammond momentary physical and emotional satisfaction, to bolster his ego, and to ingratiate him with others (note his pride at being able to show off Janey as his wife to business acquaintances under normal circumstances)—it is no wonder that her kisses are contractual and her demeanor cool and proper.

It is also interesting, as several critics have noted, that Mansfield alludes often to Hammond's heart long before the condition of the stranger's heart becomes part of the narrative.[18] A stray thought warms his heart as he stands on the crowded wharf. Holding Jean "lightened his heart." Seeing his wife on the deck affects him: "His heart was wrung with . . . a spasm" (p. 449). And he wonders even whether the boat's "deep throbbing" came from "her engines or his heart" (p. 448). Once the boat docks, his relief is intense "at being rid of that horrible tug, pull, grip on his heart" (p. 452). What Hammond doesn't know yet is that the arrival of the ship in port will signalize for him the death of his own heart—a seizure brought on by the failure of a stranger's heart—the heart of an undifferentiated fly who only the day before strolled about the deck.

In a sense, too, the dead stranger is Hammond, in terms of Janey's reaction to both men. For her solicitiousness toward the man on the ship is precisely what the reader would expect her to show toward her husband under parallel circumstances. In explaining her actions of the night before to Hammond, she stresses the objectivity and impersonality of her role. She is concerned with the propriety of allowing a man to die in the arms of a stewardess. She feels that she has fulfilled her quasi-contractual obligations to a fellow human being in need when she ministers to the sufferer—just as Hammond senses she ministers to him in their marriage—out of a sense of duty and justness rather than deep feeling. Significantly, just as there was little communication between Janey and the stranger, so there is almost none between the two Hammonds. Their conversation after almost a year of separation is singularly free from meaningful context. Hammond may be burning within for love or lust—as the fire on the hearth blazes briefly—but the couple share no common store of experiences, emotions, or thoughts. The only world they appear to have in common, the world of their children, is significantly shunted aside when he entreats his wife to wait before opening the letters from their offspring. In every regard, Hammond stands as much at a distance from Janey as the stranger on the ship did. Janey stays with the dying man because "he might have wanted to leave a message" (p. 457), but the latter dies "without a word," being "too weak" to say anything. From Hammond, whose emotional relationship with Janey is atrophying and who cannot be "*dead* certain" (p. 455) [italics mine] of his wife's feeling toward him, there is not a word either of genuine connection. "Too weak," he leans on Jean and Janey for support without being able to offer any meaningful gift in return. This "strong-looking . . . man" (p. 446) is, in effect, dead and blind to the realities of his existence and yet has not had sense enough "to bring any glasses" (p. 446). Moved only by sexual passion, he sees the double bed in their hotel room, after his epiphany, as "blind" and his "coat flung across it like some headless man" (p. 457) as significant of his position.

It has been remarked before that in this story Mansfield is particularly adept at integrating narrative and symbol so that, seemingly without effort, the physical description of people and places operates to reveal, or at least to suggest, much more than the tale appears to be saying. Most obviously, the author works with imagery of fire and chill, wetness and dryness, and the like. Thus, Hammond imagines when the ship docks that "the danger was over" because they were "on dry land again"

(p. 452). He fails to see that much of his fantasy regarding the idyllic relationship he presumably enjoys with his wife comes from her being away, on the water, and that the return to dry land is a return to the aridity of a dead marriage—one from which the last drops of romance and spontaneous love have been squeezed. The danger is, ironically, in the *return* to dry land and to the reunion with the husband who arrives at the wharf with "his folded umbrella."

Mansfield gives most elaborate treatment to the hot-cold cluster of allusions. Almost the first thing the reader learns about Janey is that she possesses a "cool little voice" (p. 450). And the voice is typical of the rest of her. Utterly self-contained, primly detached, belonging to everyone because she truly belongs to nobody, she gives her husband the impression that "he was holding something that never was quite his" (p. 453). As the couple approaches their hotel room, the reader learns that Hammond has ordered a fire lest his wife feel "chilly" (p. 453). As Hammond "shepherded" Janey in (as earlier his looks had shepherded strangers on the wharf), "the fire blazed" (p. 454). The flush on his face and the passion in his heart match the redness of the flames as he asks Janey to sit on his knee before the fire. When the children's letters to their mother intrude on his passion, he is for chucking them "into the fire" (p. 455), sacrificing this rival relationship to his obsessive need. Shortly afterward, as she tells Hammond of her role with the heart victim, she sees the "fire flicker and fall." Passion dissipates, and her words, "so chill, seemed to hover in the air, to rain into his breast like snow" (p. 457). Simultaneously the embers in the fireplace fall and the room becomes cold. As he holds the now silent Janey, "cold crept up his arms" (p. 457). The revelation has made him weak, old, virtually dead.

Mansfield was to strike this motif of estrangement, of

loneliness in the most intimate of human relationships, again and again in the final disillusioned years of her short life. In "Bliss," the stranger is ostensibly Miss Fulton, who comes to intrude upon the connection between Harry and Bertha—a connection which the reader discovers, in spite of the wife's protestations of marital euphoria, is not there to begin with. In "Marriage à la Mode," the stranger is the entire bohemian clique which imposes itself and usurps the place of the husband in a relationship too fragile to be sustained. In each instance the havoc wrought by the outsider could not have occurred if the original emotional attachment had been deep and vital. The failure is always that of one or both partners to offer appropriate emotional sustenance to the other—rather than the positive inroads of third parties bent on destroying a marriage. Though Antony Alpers traces the origin of "The Stranger" to Mansfield's memories of her mother and father,[19] a closer analogy may be the author's own estrangements in two marital situations.

"A Dill Pickle," largely ignored or patronized by critics, reveals Mansfield on the brink of maturity. Fewer than seven pages in length, it yet establishes vividly the essence of a man and a woman, suggests the past, dramatizes the present, and implies the future by severe verbal economy and the sure employment of metaphorical devices hitherto reserved to poets like Eliot and Pound, whose portraits of ladies are called to mind.

An entry in Mansfield's *Journal* may have been the point of departure for the plot. On August 21, 1917, Mansfield writes:

I came home this afternoon and F. came in. . . . By and by we sat down and had tea and talk. This man is in many ways extraordinarily like me. I like him so much; I feel so *honest* with him. . . . I did not realize, until he was here and we ate together, how much I cared for him. . . . A real understanding. We might have spoken a different language—returned from a far country. I just felt all was well, and we understood each other. . . .

We said good-bye at Vinden's. That is all. But I wanted to make a note of it.

I. They meet and just touch.
II. They come together and part.
III. They are separated and meet again.
IV. They realize their tie.[20]

All that Mansfield needed to add to this bare outline is the fifth step of "A Dill Pickle": They also realize their incompatibility and therefore part.

The fashion in which the author transforms this simple narrative line—highly sentimental and almost banal—into a successful short story merits more attention than it has received. The story is built upon a then-and-now polarity, and the incidents move rapidly from one pole to the other. Connecting the two poles is a kind of perfume of relationship—a tenuous yet vividly recurring series of sense relationships that the author from time to time introduces. The peeling of an orange in an Oriental cafe recalls a similar manner of peeling fruit in earlier days. The present eating place with the Japanese vase and bamboo tables sets the woman's mind to thinking of an earlier scene in a Chinese pagoda tea shop. The paper daffodils on the table now are balanced by the real flowers the two admired in Kew Gardens years before.

It is almost as though the ability to enjoy, or to have enjoyed, this pleasure of the senses is directly related to the possibility of human compatibility. Thus, the man elicits from Vera the admission that she has given up the making of music:

"Do you ever play it now?"
"No, I've no piano."

He was amazed at that. "But what has become of your beautiful piano?"

She made a little grimace. "Sold. Ages ago." (p. 333)

He remembers their visit to Kew Gardens on a "very fine and warm" (p. 332) day, but now Vera's principal concern appears to be the avoidance of the sensation of cold. Her high fur, her muff, her gloves, and all her thoughts on the weather attest to her apprehension. For her, the colorful and fragrant true flowers of the Gardens have been replaced by the "paper daffodils" (p. 330) of the restaurant, and even in breathing the air round these artificial flowers, she inhales "as though the paper daffodils between them were almost too sweet to bear" (p. 332). Nor does she answer the man's question when he asks whether she is "still so fond of perfumes" (p. 333) as in the old days. Instead she interrupts his question as he in earlier days had been accustomed to breaking in on her conversation.

The man, on the other hand, appears at least to savor the joys of the senses and thus to be ready now for human connection as he was not ready six years before. Mansfield has taken pains to delineate him as a younger man and a rather selfish, foolish person. His immature confession of a wish to die lest his growing love for Vera cause him pain is an obvious effort to mark his unwillingness for involvement. And the rather "absurd scene" in the Chinese tea shop when he behaves like a "maniac" (p. 332) in his frenzy to escape being stung by wasps further stresses his wish to avoid physical sensation—this time painful without the concomitant enjoyment of pleasure.

Now, however, the man has had six years of experience with life since his last encounter with Vera, six years in which to change. The alteration seems apparent. He enjoys, ostensibly, "the warm, stinging scent of the orange peel" (p. 331). He recalls the colors and the names of the flowers they visited together. He considers smoking "delicious, very fresh cigarettes" a "luxury," and he talks of perfume, exotic places, and music.

These references in the story, scattered though they are, are central in importance, and they lead as they ought to a discussion of connection by the man. Speaking of his days on a river boat on the Volga River, he concludes that "the life of the boat creates a bond between you and the people that's more than sufficient" (p. 334). He reminds her that "it is not necessary to know the language" (p. 334), a particularly apposite reflection in the light of their own relationship, spoiled six years before by the words of a letter the woman had sent him and about to be spoiled again by the man's carelessly uttered remarks about his companion. A connection deeper than words can produce is made between the man and his Russian coachman (different from him in nationality, language, social class, and environment) by the coachman's offer of a dill pickle at a picnic on the Black Sea. It will be noted that the offer is of a particularly tantalizing, sharp sense experience that only eating a pickle provides. Yet Vera is "not certain what a dill pickle was" and only vicariously "sucked in her cheeks; the dill pickle was terrible sour . . ." (p. 334) [ellipsis marks Mansfield's]. Even at secondhand, this taste of life and involvement for Vera is "sour," for it would force her to forego her protective covering of gloves, muff, and the rest, for the dangers of exposure to life's sharp sensations. No wonder, then, with the realization that she is "as alone as ever" (p. 337), she disappears from the table and from her companion to avoid commitment.

The ending of the story is puzzling. The man reminds the waitress that he does not want to be charged for the cream inasmuch as it has not been consumed. The attempt seems to be to show that he has not changed greatly since the day, six years earlier, when he expressed shock that Vera would pay seven and sixpence for a tiny portion of caviar. It is quite possible that this throwback in behavior to a former period would not have occurred had he not been deserted again by Vera—that six years of advancing maturity had been temporarily sloughed off by a repetition of the traumatic situation and that his concluding remark is meant to illustrate the reassumption of his earlier stance. This view is partially reinforced by the fact that just prior to his remark to the waitress, he has been talking at great length to a companion who is no longer there. The realization of his present role puts him precisely where he was before the experience of the dill pickle. To Vera also had come the realization that, except superficially, things had not changed for either of them.

One of the stories on which Katherine Mansfield's reputation as an artist chiefly rests is "The Garden Party," which she completed on October 14, 1921. Aside from its merits as fiction, it provides an opportunity for its author to be at once her satirical earlier self, the gentle recorder of her New Zealand childhood, and the new, transfigured personality whose view of life is complex, warm, and utterly philosophical. Without self-consciousness, she writes to William Gerhardi in 1922 that she has tried to express in the story

> the diversity of life and how we try to fit in everything, Death included. That is bewildering for a person of Laura's age. She feels things ought to happen differently. First one and then another. But life isn't like that. We haven't the ordering of it. Laura says, "But all these things must not happen at once." And Life answers, "Why not? How are they divided from each other?" And they *do* all happen, it is inevitable. And it seems to me there is beauty in that inevitability.[21]

Perhaps it is unfortunate that critics of "The Garden Party" have dwelt so extensively on this excerpt from

Mansfield's letter, for they have generally tended to see the story almost exclusively as a reconciliation of Death and Life: that is, the parenthetical "Death included" has been read as though it were "Death especially." Rather, the attempt is equally to reconcile reality and the dream, innocence and experience, and, with great concern, levels of society. That Mansfield could even hope to carry out so ambitious an enterprise within the limitations of the short story is testimony to the increasing self-confidence that she felt during the last year of her life.

The story itself seems simple, childishly unsophisticated, even obvious, but this view proves untenable. The narrative involves preparations for a garden party—Laura's first grown-up affair; a glimpse of the party itself; and the aftermath which describes an impulsive attempt to give the party leftovers to the bereaved family of an accident victim. Mansfield's "selective camera" [22] centers upon Laura, a young and wellmeaning girl trying to establish her own values in a world carefully arranged for her by the women in her family: her mother Mrs. Sheridan and her two older sisters. The camera follows Laura as she adopts the ways of her mother in talking to the workmen or to her friend Kitty; as she helps with the sandwiches; and as she confronts the insensitivity of her elders to the death which has happened nearby. The reader notes her wavering allegiance to the attitude of the family and, on the other hand, to her instinctive youthful sense of proportion and good taste that assumes the cancellation of the party out of respect for the other family's grief. The devices employed to divert Laura from her independent point of view and to set her firmly once again in the Sheridan orbit are described. The story ends with her visit to the home of the dead man bearing the party leftovers and with her enchantment with the appearance of death as she views the body. Her final "Isn't life . . . isn't life" (p. 649) represents not nearly as ambiguous and inconclusive an ending as has been charged to the author, but a deeper look at the story is necessary to demonstrate this.

Mansfield's choice of a garden party as the focus of action and attitude is obviously meaningful.[23] No less than Joyce, who praised Ibsen for using "never a superfluous word or phrase,"[24] Katherine Mansfield insists on the inevitability of all elements in a successful story. (Her remarks on the writing of "Miss Brill" are particularly relevant here.)[25] Clearly, a garden party offered the author a many-faceted symbol. Thus it may represent the Sheridan way of life: showy, superficial, upper class, ephemeral (almost before final preparations are made for the affair comes a description of its aftermath), and with little more substance than the cream puffs that are served. In a wider sense, the garden party is life itself, the brief moment men enjoy between cradle and grave. Perhaps this is why Mansfield required a party in the garden rather than in the drawing room of the Sheridan home. For a garden implies nature and natural development, a developing and growing into maturity, and, inevitably too, a withering and dying. It is no accident either that Laura's own name has associations with a growing plant or that, when the florist delivers a profusion of lilies to augment the attractions of the garden flowers, Laura "felt they were in her fingers, on her lips, growing in her breast" (p. 538).

Employment of the garden as a symbol of life, of natural growth and development, permits Mansfield to play upon the perversion of the natural too—whether with respect to nature or to man. Thus, in the first paragraph of the story, before the reader is introduced specifically to any character or to details of plot, the point of view of the opening description suggests the unnaturalness of what is to occur in a "natural" setting. Probably at Mrs. Sheridan's suggestion, the gardener has been "mowing the lawns and sweeping them" until the grass "seemed to shine" (p. 534). This attempt to "methodize" nature and bring it under control is implicit also in the line: "They could not have had a more perfect day for a garden-party *if they had ordered it*" (p. 534) [italics mine], in which climatic conditions are reduced to a matter of commercial transaction. Further, perhaps the height of perversity is reached in the turn of mind which conceives of roses blooming precisely in time for the party because they are the flowers most likely to "impress people at garden-parties" (p. 534) and the roses know it. The horror is that the point of view here must be attributed to the young and innocent Laura, though the reader quickly senses that the hands guiding the strings are the hands of the mother. Similarly, later in the story young Kitty Maitland's plans for the "green-coated band" bespeak the insensitivity of the older generation: "Aren't they too like frogs for words? You ought to have arranged them round the pond with the conductor in the middle on a leaf" (p. 544).

This afternoon affair is Laura's coming-out party—the first social occasion on which she is to play an adult role. It is, as others have pointed out, her initiation into the mature world. If she has hitherto been merely a bud on the parent stem, on this day she will have her opportunity to blossom. The question is, of course, whether she will grow into a simple, natural flower or whether, like her mother, she is doomed to artificiality, insensitivity, and falseness. The restricted view of the world that she and her sisters have been permitted by their mother has already made inroads into her spontaneity and natural freshness, as the first paragraph abundantly proves. Without a dramatic widening of horizons to force a reevaluation of basic elements, Laura's path, following in the footsteps of Meg and Jose and her mother, is clearly predictable.

Death makes the difference and, at least temporarily, forces Laura to see in the older women in her family the crystallized and hardened views which in herself are still vague and indefinite imitations of adult models. The most final of all human activities makes her own growth and development less certain than it was that morning. Knowledge of death means an end to innocence but it also heralds the possibility of a new kind of life. The death of Scott the carter postpones maybe forever the death of the heart in Laura—a death already suffered by the other Sheridan women.

Yet if the death itself and the subsequent reactions to it of the Sheridans can accomplish this new healthy growth for Laura, why does Mansfield bother to include the last section of the story? Is it necessary for Laura to see a corpse in order for the meaning of the day's lesson to sink in? Or can Mansfield not resist the emotional value of a child's confrontation with the physical presence of death? The answers to these questions require examination of the story from another point of view.

On the day of the party, Laura loses her innocence and her parent-fostered narrowness in more ways than one. The development of her attitude toward class distinction accelerates as the day advances, further widening the gap between her and the other Sheridan women. The progress of the development is put by Mansfield in terms of Laura's increasing difficulty in generalizing about the working-class group of whose lives she knows almost nothing as the story opens. Subtly, Mansfield encourages the reader to accept Laura's sterotyped impression of the workmen who have come to put up the marquee:

> Four men in their shirt-sleeves stood grouped together on the garden path. They carried staves . . . and they had big

tool-bags slung on their backs. They looked impressive. (p. 535)

Through the repetition of "they," through the monotony of sentence structure and word order, and through her underlining of the fact that these shirt-sleeved men were "grouped together," Mansfield reinforces the generalization almost schematically, as though picturing on a social studies graph the distribution of laborers in the locality. And, though Laura welcomes contact with this rarely encountered group, she embraces the generalization enthusiastically. If *a* workman has nice eyes, the corollary is "How very nice work*men* were" (p. 535) [italics mine]. When an individual workman uses slang in conversing with her, she wonders whether such talk is quite respectful of *a* workman. When one smells a sprig of lavender, she approves of all workmen at the expense of all "the silly boys" of her own class at dances. And when in the garden she takes a bite of bread-and-butter, she feels "just like a work-girl" (p. 536).

Death, the Great Leveller, succeeds in making Laura wary of generalizations. Suddenly the girl who in the garden that morning could react only on that level discovers that in her elders' resort to generalization is a method of avoiding unpleasant confrontations, mental or physical—and her natural honesty is shocked into an awareness of the immorality of the process. To her sister's "You won't bring a drunken workman back to life by being sentimental," she counters, "Drunk! Who said he was drunk?" (p. 542). She is similarly outraged when her mother speaks nebulously of not understanding how "they" keep alive "in those poky little holes" (p. 543).

But to Laura, if not to her family, a dead workman cannot be generalized away. In bringing the news of the accident, Godber's man has been deliberately particular.

Though the dead man is hardly a character in the story, the protagonist and the reader are given his name, his profession, the nature of the accident, the name of the street on which it occurred, the location of the wound, his marital status, and the number of his children. Such detailed categorization is essential to the breaking down in Laura of the vague barrier between class and class. Now it is easier to see why Laura must make the post-party trip to Scott's cottage and look upon the carter not as just another dead workman to be subtracted from census statistics, but as an individual being. It becomes clear why Laura must ask the woman who opens the door at Scott's home whether she is Mrs. Scott and why she must discover that the woman is not. Identities count now, even among workpeople.

The final step in Laura's development on this day is her reaction to the dead Scott. He now transends class. As Laura had lived in a different world from workmen hitherto, Scott inhabits a dream realm which removes him, in a sense, from his own former slum world and from her world too. His is the classless world of death to which Mrs. Sheridan and Mrs. Scott and Jose and Laura–everyone–must eventually come. It is no wonder that Laura's response to this new "marvel" should be a tearful, "Forgive my hat" (p. 548).

Hats had dominated the story as one image followed another from the beginning: the turban Meg wears, Laurie and his father brushing their hats, the carelessly worn hats of the workmen, Kitty Maitland's hat, and finally the hat of Laura's mother, hastily "popped" on her head by Mrs. Sheridan to make Laura forget the dead man and her opposition to holding the garden party. When the mother thus presents her daughter with her own party hat in typical coronation fashion, she is symbolically transferring to Laura the Sheridan heritage of snobbery, restricted social views, narrowness of vision—the garden party syndrome. It is not surprising that when Laura first sees herself in a mirror wearing the hat, she hardly recognizes "this charming girl" (p. 543) who stares back at her. Certainly the hat is, as her mother tells her, "made for" her, but she is not at all sure that she wishes to acquire her rightful legacy. In the presence of Scott, the realization of the discrepancy between what the hat indicates and what Laura in her own dawning maturity is tending toward evokes the involuntary cry. Laura has had her vision.

As several critics have shown, Mansfield has prepared the reader for this epiphany through earlier introducing the "This Life is Weary" song, whose tragic burden evokes only a "brilliant, dreadfully unsympathetic smile" (p. 539) from the singer herself. The final line, "A Dream—a *Wa*-kening," is echoed in the description of Scott at the end of the story: "He was dreaming. Never wake him up again" (p. 548). In a sense, Laura has through contact with death wakened from her dream-life, the existence of garden parties and Sheridan exclusivity. And Scott has, in her eyes, awakened through death to a life infinitely more desirable than that of the Sheridans. Both have a knowledge that puts them above class.

It is almost as though Katherine Mansfield dangles obscurely before the reader the dim symbol of another garden—a false Eden this time—a dream world of artificial delight and false security. The inhabitants of this fools' paradise tend the garden, "order" the appropriate weather, and regard themselves as the center of the universe. Only when Laura is expelled from the garden does she trade innocence for knowledge. Now she can see death in the world and "all our woe," unwarned not to resist by the "archangels" who Mansfield tells us had visited the garden on the evening before the party. Yet the confrontation with death is to the awakened Laura not only not frightening: it is positively an ecstatic experience. For her protagonist at least, Mansfield has been able to demonstrate that life and death may indeed coexist and that their common existence in one world may be beautiful.

The final scene with Laurie appears much less ambiguous than critics have allowed. The fairylike Laura who had, before the fact of death entered her life, dealt with life largely in terms of comfortable generalizations, finds herself speechless now to sum up the complexity that the deeper view affords. When she stammers, "Isn't life—?" the generalizing predicate adjective will not come, for no single word can encompass it. It would not matter, in this regard, whether the question were completed by "good" or "bad," "ugly" or "beautiful, "sad" or "happy." What matters is that no one word suffices in a world that encompasses, though it may not always reconcile, all of them.

The unspoken communication here between Laura and Laurie is interesting. Laurie "quite understood" (p. 549) although she "couldn't explain." Mansfield chooses to associate brother and sister closely not only in their ages ostensibly, but in Laurie's sympathy for his sister's point of view and his apparent humanity when contrasted with the female Sheridans' coldness. Furthermore, by calling them Laura and Laurie, the author establishes an obvious similiarity. It may be that they are intended to be male and female aspects of the same personality and that, therefore, their reactions would be identical. It is not necessary, though it is possible, to believe with one critic that Laurie had earlier been initiated into knowledge of death and thus can emphathize with the new initiate.

Katherine Mansfield considered "The Garden Party" "moderately successful,"[26] but had reservations about the quality of the ending. She had worked on parts of it during a period of at least five months, as her *Scrapbook* shows, though the episode given there in an earlier form survives in "The Garden Party" as the song "This Life is Weary" and as very little else.[27] Called "By Moonlight" in the *Scrapbook*, the episode of the song is treated discursively for over three pages as the focal point for a view of the Sheridans: "Mother," "Father," Meg, Laura, Laurie, and Francie (the Jose of the later story). Since there is no garden party and no dead man in the sketch, the significance of the song is considerably less, its employment being confined to pointing up attitudes of those who hear it. "Mother" especially is revealed as she deplores the trend toward the "tragic" and the "depressing" in contemporary lyrics. She states her preference for "songs about primroses and cheerful normal birds and . . . [ellipsis marks Mansfield's] and spring and so on." Thus the morbid and the lower class are excluded from her world here as they will be later in the "Garden party" story. As for Meg, she finds the song "fascinating." But to the reader, the fascination is in seeing how Mansfield surrounds the song with meaning in the later version as she is unable to do a few weeks earlier.[28]

6

Katherine Mansfield: The Summing Up

In a moment of private pique, Virginia Woolf confided to her diary on August 7, 1918, her objections to Mansfield as woman and artist:

> I threw down [Katherine Mansfield's] *Bliss* with the exclamation, "She's done for!" Indeed I don't see how much faith in her as woman or writer can survive that sort of story. I shall have to accept the fact, I'm afraid, that her mind is a very thin soil, laid an inch or two deep upon very barren rock. For *Bliss* is long enough to give her a chance of going deeper. Instead she is content with superficial smartness; and the whole conception is poor, cheap, not the vision, however imperfect, of an interesting mind. She writes badly too.

The effect of reading the story is to "give me an impression of her callousness and hardness as a human being," though Woolf tempers this final judgment with the worried thought, "Or is it absurd to read all this criticism of her personally into a story?" [1] Though the reader may harbor his own doubts of the critical solidity of Woolf's private outburst, the recently published diary entry offers a point of departure for an assessment of Mansfield's strengths and weaknesses as a writer.

To the charge that Mansfield's mind is "a very thin soil, laid . . . upon very barren rock," little can be said in reply. Mansfield is clearly of a different order than Tolstoy, who possessed, according to Woolf, a "rugged short cut mind—to me the most, not sympathetic, but inspiring, rousing: genius in the raw."[2] Sick and invalided in her twenties, dead in her early thirties, the writer of "Bliss" had neither the time nor the opportunity to develop her mind in the ordinary channels. For most of her adult life, the salons of Bloomsbury were a continent away as she sought the south of France for the improvement of her health. Nor was she fortunate enough to encounter the French or Swiss intelligentsia during her enforced stays in those countries. Her complaint in letter after letter to Murry is that she is alone, dreadfully solitary in her hotel room, and that the vulgar, mean, stupid middle-class Frenchmen (whom she came to loathe) offered no relief from her isolation. Some of her stories reflect her situation: the relationship between the mistress and her lady's maid. Many of the stories are set in hotel rooms and deal in one way or another with the loneliness of the protagonist.[3] Add to the isolation and the distance from an intellectual center Mansfield's natural concern with her own failing body and her likely early death and the wonder is that she was able to practice her craft with as much mental agility as she shows.

It must be remembered too that Mansfield's educational opportunities were quite ordinary. After her formal education at what today would be considered a young lady's finishing school, her reading was haphazard. Often, during her years abroad, she read the books that were sent to her for review, or an occasional book sent to her for comment by an author acquaintance. Occasionally, she requested that Murry send her a specific work, but more often she relied on chance to set the course of her intellectual stimulation. So niggling a consideration as money sometimes dictated what her mind might be exposed to and what not. In the light of such a background, her acute interest in such a work as *Cosmic Anatomy*[4] no longer seems perverse.

In a sense, a part of Katherine Mansfield's being never grew up beyond the point it had reached about a decade before her death. Like Wordsworth, invalided and isolated, she nurtured her youthful experience and made it the center of her later work in fiction. The depiction of children—herself and those she had known—became her trademark. The impinging of the real world of ugliness and perversion on the paradise of childhood innocence is as strong in a later work like "The Garden Party" as it is in an early story like "The Little Governess." The relationship of men to women, dealt with in detail in an earlier chapter, comes down always in Mansfield's fiction to the childhood fear of abandonment. In "A Dill Pickle," the original abandonment is repeated at the end, in "Psychology," the woman takes steps in the last paragraph to ensure against future loss of her male friend. "The Man Without a Temperament" grapples with the theme, as do many other stories. It is true that, with chronological maturity, the motif is enriched far beyond the unsophisticated treatment it receives in "Something Childish But Very Natural"; yet the enrichment seems one of technique and literary experience rather than the result of enhanced intellectual depth. Even the fear of impending death—the subject of several stories—is handled unphilosophically, as a physical terror to be approached hysterically.

In Mansfield's letters especially, it is interesting to note that her childlike chirpiness continues from the earliest letter to Murry in the volume (Summer 1913) to the letters of the last months. Though Mansfield has aged and degenerated physically, she strains to keep the young note in her most personal utterances:

I'm very happy, darling. But when you come into my thoughts I refuse you, quickly, quickly. It would take me a long time away from you before I could bear to think of you. You see, when I am not with you, every little bit of you puts out a flaming sword.[5]

Compare this letter of 1913 with the following written in November 1920:

You are my Boge, my "veen" (whoever he is, he's *very* important) you are also Basil-love and Jag-Boge. If you were here, you would believe me. When you come, you will! You *are* coming at Xmas? I am preparing for you every single day.[6]

The immaturity of mind which Woolf perceives in Mansfield's work, then, is real and does lead in her art to a rather circumscribed, shallow choice of subject materials. It leads to a dramatization in fiction of the chief concerns of a sensitive invalid: the reconstruction of a happier past of childhood memories, fear of abandonment by loved ones, fear of death as an imminent probability, fear of loneliness and isolation, and occasional projections into fictional situations of wish-fulfillment. Though Mansfield approves of Chekhov's admonition to writers to stand apart from their work, to keep their hands and feet hidden, and though she is able technically to follow his instructions in the literary style of her presentation, yet in all but a few stories (like "The Daughters of the Late Colonel" and perhaps "Je ne parle pas français") the Mansfield presence is strongly felt. The problems of the protagonists are her problems and the resolution is sensed as a very personal resolution for the author as well. Katherine Mansfield grasps intellectually Chekhov's advice to deal with icy coldness in in matters of fiery concern, but emotionally the identification is made.

Virginia Woolf criticizes Mansfield's "superficial smartness," and complains that the "whole conception" of "Bliss" is "poor, cheap, not the vision, however imperfect, of an interesting mind." The analysis of this story in an earlier chapter may in part refute the charge of superficiality of conception. On the other hand, matters of symbolic intent and the patterning of characters in intricate arrangement aside, undoubtedly Mansfield's attitude toward the short story does fall short of the intellectual expectations of an author who had published *The Voyage Out* just three years earlier and who was to publish *Night and Day* within the year. For Woolf, the development of Rachel Vinrace is simply a center about which to construct a many-faceted view of a changing world: Freud, feminism, the relationship of men and women in our time, the philosophy of history, imperialism, the nature of love, and life, and death—as the mind examines them.

To Mansfield "Love is glorified childhood,"[7] and, with equal simplicity and naïveté, most subjects may be examined in fiction with the wide-open, uncomplicated gaze of a child. Such a course eliminates the likelihood of philosophical consideration, effectively reduces history to the immediate present, and denies the validity of relevant intellectual speculation in the fiction itself. This is why, perhaps, Mansfield is especially successful in her presentation of children, where the subject matter fits the tone precisely; and why, on the other hand, stories like "This Flower" and "The Escape" and "Mr. and Mrs. Dove" suffer from treatment too one-dimensional and simplistic. It is not surprising that the daughter of Leslie Stephen found Mansfield's mind not "interesting."

Had Woolf been commenting on a less ambitious story than "Bliss," she might have found Mansfield's manner more childish than childlike. Especially in the early *German Pension* stories, Mansfield's "cuteness" of manner can destroy the carefully drawn sketches that she displays. The final line of "Sister of the Baroness" is a useless flourish: "Tableau grandissimo!" (p. 49). "The

Baron" ends with comic strip flippancy: "Next day the Baron was gone. Sic transit gloria German mundi" (p. 44). And even her most distinguished stories, like "The Daughters of the Late Colonel," which is written ten years later, do not avoid preadolescent cleverness:

> Josephine was furious. "Oh, what nonsense, Con!" she said. "What have mice got to do with it? You're asleep."
>
> "I don't think I am," said Constantia. She shut her eyes to make sure. *She was.* [italics mine] (p. 465)

With all her pruning and revision, Mansfield was unable always to avoid sounding like a child showing off before a doting audience.

Yet, granting all these deficiencies of mind and matter, the reader of the stories acknowledges Katherine Mansfield as an authentic voice in contemporary fiction. It is more difficult to account for her artistic success than to isolate her weaknesses.

A heightened sensitivity to personal relationships in fiction is perhaps Mansfield's foremost asset as a writer of short stories. Forced to conduct most of her own meaningful relationships through correspondence, the lonely author apparently turned to artistic account her private deprivations. Her analyses of the emotional lives of her characters in interaction with other characters seem invariably precise and normally the result of intuitive judgment. What gives "The Stranger" and "The Man Without a Temperament" their power is Mansfield's unerring portrayal of the marriage relationship, very different in each instance but both entirely right for the respective husbands and wives. In "Prelude" and "At the Bay," the delineation of the major characters, though often remarkable in the short space at the author's disposal, is less impressive than her power to represent the separate characters in their interrelationship. Beryl is one kind of human being to Linda, another to Stanley, and still a third to Kezia. Yet she remains consistently believable to all the other characters, and to the reader, as Beryl. What Mansfield has accomplished in these two stories intuitively in the way of character development and the interaction of characters, Virginia Woolf was to attempt years later with intellectual precision and conscious cerebration in *The Waves.*

In addition, borrowing mainly from the Russian writers of fiction, Mansfield pioneered in verbalizing the relationship of a character to himself (or perhaps to his other self). In the tradition of Conrad's "Secret Sharer," Dostoyevsky's disturbed student-murderer, is Beryl once more, writing a letter to her friend Nan, and then standing to one side as she recognizes that the writer is truly another part of herself. Mansfield's treatment of this theme is less enterprising than Conrad's but much less obvious and artificial. True to her own critical tenets as expressed in numerous reviews of novels in the *Athenaeum,*[8] she never allows her handling of the psychology of human relationships to degenerate into disguised lectures on psychoanalysis or undigested gobbets of scientific theory. The author keeps her eye on the character as fictional human being first of all—and only incidentally on the psychology textbook.

Virginia Woolf's complaint that Katherine Mansfield "writes badly" requires qualification. The latter set aside most of her waking hours during the greater portion of her adult life to the craft of the short story. Unconcerned with quantity, she devoted herself painstakingly to the writing of less than one hundred stories, pushing herself unremittingly to produce the highest degree of artistry of which she might be capable. Owing to her insistence that early drafts and revisions of her work not be preserved, the critic is in most instances not able to examine the successive steps in the creation of her fiction. Where an early draft is available, as with *The Aloe* and "Prelude," it is clear that the artist scrutinized every word and every punctuation mark of the first version in forming the final story. The critic has in addition occasional statements in Mansfield's letters attesting to the care she took to employ not merely the essential words in a story, but the rhythms and the sounds of the sentences themselves. All these evidences of care in the details of composition do not necessarily refute the charge that Mansfield "writes badly," but they do demonstrate that any failing in her art is not the result of carelessness or a slipshod approach, or haste, or, most important, lack of critical standards. Mansfield knew what she wanted to do in fiction, and went about doing it in a precise and deliberate way.

One of her aims was to use the image and the symbol as meaningfully in prose fiction as her predecessors and contemporaries were employing it in poetry. Her ability thus to portray a truth of life by indirection, incidentally as it were, while the narrative level of the story remained simple and one-dimensional, is perhaps her major contribution to the modern short story. A simple statement of the triangle-situation of "Bliss" conveys no more than may be read on page three of any tabloid. What gives the action significance beyond itself are the symbolic reverberations arising from Mansfield's introduction of pear tree and moon, cats and gardens, food as sexual feast. The other major stories show much the same concern of Mansfield to ground an uninspired "plot" in a tight imagistic and symbolic framework so that the ordinary will be transmuted into the artistically meaningful. The examination of Mansfield's short stories in the earlier chapters of this book make further examples superfluous here.

In carrying out her elaborate symbolic design, however, Katherine Mansfield was not uniformly and skillfully subtle. Like Conrad Aiken, who was also experimenting with symbolic representation in fiction, she occasionally went beyond delicate insinuation to provide the insensitive reader with blatantly garish clues to the author's intent. Thus, when Bertha Young, in "Bliss," goes to meet her dinner guests, she wears

> a white dress, a string of jade beads, green shoes and stockings. . . . She had thought of this scheme hours before she stood at the drawing-room window [looking out at the pear tree]. (p. 342)

And as she moves, "her petals rustled softly into the hall." This overemphasis on symbolic equivalencies, natural in Aiken and Mansfield as innovators in contemporary short stories in English, probably offended Virginia's Woolf's sense of balance in art and elicited the diary charge of bad writing. Half a century later, it may be seen as stylistically unfortunate but, at the same time, historically justifiable in that innovators tend generally to exaggerate what is distinctively unusual in their treatment of literature. One finds the same urge toward explicitness in Conrad's handling of the symbolism of "The Secret Sharer" and "The Lagoon," while the manifestoes of naturalists ridiculously overstate the case for their school. Woolf might have pointed to other equally awkward instances of employment of the symbolic technique in "The Garden Party" (the number of times the "hat" motif is reiterated, for instance), or in "Something Childish But Very Natural" (the overinsistent dependence on images of nature—flowers, insects, gardens, verdant groves). Yet only by excessive emphasis on these images and symbols could Mansfield have been sure she was bringing to the awareness of her readers—most of them unused to such indirection—what the meaning of the work of art required. Significantly, in her last stories Mansfield apparently finds less need to call special attention to the symbolic framework, either because she has greater faith in her audience's ability to understand implicit allusions or because she is willing to take the chance of imperfect comprehension in order to write stories that are more nearly perfect technically. The point is not how often she is heavy-handed in the process of suggestion, but rather how often, as in "The Daughters of the Late Colonel," she maintains the delicate balance between statement and indirect evocation.

"The Fly" exemplifies a very late attempt on Katherine Mansfield's part to withdraw completely and allow the symbols to carry the entire weight of meaning. Refusing to belabor the obvious in this seven-page story, she has been so successful at indirection and insinuation that critics still argue over the point of "The Fly."[9] From R. W. Stallman's view that the theme of "The Fly" is that "Time conquers grief," expressed in *The Explicator* in 1945, to Ted E. Boyle's "The Death of the Boss: Another Look at Katherine Mansfield's 'The Fly'" in *Modern Fiction Studies* in 1965, which sees the story as the "spiritual death of the boss," conflicting views have proliferated. At least one attempt has been made to ascribe autobiographical significances to the weakened insect destroyed by the insensitive bank manager: namely, Mansfield the invalid destroyed by her banker father. That Mansfield's very short story should have received such full-dress treatment over so long a period is testimony to the imaginative hold her symbolic fiction exerts on the critical mind.

In "The Fly," suggesting more than is said is accomplished through symbolic reference. Mansfield is adept at other techniques of suggestion too. In "Marriage à la Mode," myth and literary allusion play their parts as Titania and Oberon, sifted through Shakespeare, broaden the domestic tragicomedy at the same time as they reduce the contemporary husband and wife and their court of merrymakers to pygmy size. In "Miss

Brill," the technique to to juxtapose the young, vital, physically attractive pair of lovers to the bloodless, withered Miss Brill in such a way that the elderly protagonist realizes her own epiphany and harvests only bitterness. The fact that these stories are particularly short suggests the author's heightened ability to work with fewer words to attain far more powerful effects than in the earlier, longer stories.

Katherine Mansfield's fiction is important also for its ability to verbalize dramatically levels of consciousness seldom depicted effectively in English short fiction up to her time. In "The Wrong House"—a story less than three pages in length—Mansfield conveys the chilling terror that the elderly Mrs. Bean feels when a funeral coach stops mistakenly at the door of her own house. Her epiphany is never rendered explicitly. Instead, the author describes—depicts, rather—the protagonist's almost speechless shock at the morticians' error, followed by her successive stages on the road back to emotional normality: her realization that her servant woman has returned to provide human companionship, her calling for "the lamp" to banish the shadows of oncoming night and fear, her return to her knitting but with a reversal of the knitting pattern, and, eventually, her renewed interest in physical existence as she admonishes the servant not to "forget the mace" in preparing the chicken for the evening meal. In this tiny story of 1919, Mansfield shows herself to be as skillful a manipulator of the technique of epiphany as Joyce was in fiction of comparable texture. Nor is "The Wrong House" unique: the critic might with equal justice have cited "Her First Ball," or "The Doll's House," or "The Young Girl."

Katherine Mansfield is helped in her fiction by her adherence to her own unities of time and place. Almost all of the stories run their course within rigid boundaries of chronology and setting. Often the rigidity of these elements is not immediately apparent because the author, like Virginia Woolf, has learned how to manipulate time and place through the medium of memory or of daydream. As "The Daughters of the Late Colonel" has shown, time may even become a participant in the story, and the manipulation of time past and time future in relation to the time present of the main action may render that main action more significant. Thus, Mansfield can have her unity and yet bring to bear on it the enrichment of simultaneous juxtaposition of past and future too. "Bliss," "Miss Brill," and "The Stranger" afford illustrations of this technique.

Katherine Mansfield is not a great writer, though in a very few stories she approaches artistry of the first rank. Her significance to the contemporary critic is as an authentic and original talent in fiction. Like Virginia Woolf in the novel, Mansfield felt the need to break windows. Her emulation of her Russian predecessors in her inimitable English prose helped alter the reading tastes of an English public surrounded by insipidity and pretension in the short fiction available at the time of the First World War. Like Joseph Conrad and James Joyce, she wrote at a time when a breakthrough in the representation of reality was not only desirable but also possible in the English short story: when the tools of psychology might be employed to construct meaningful symbolic structures in fiction; and when literary characters might be examined from the inside as well as from the outside, whole or fragmented into aspects of themselves. She wrote at a time when the furniture of fiction was largely being scrapped in favor of concentration on essences: the spirit that moved human beings rather than the scene in which they moved. Her recognition of these new directions came early. Her determination to follow them, not as a member of a coterie but because she understood that they were the only paths open to her kind of talent, has assured her a small but secure place in literary history. Much more than the influence of her literary criticism, her short stories have played a large part in shaping the contemporary short story in our language.

But Mansfield does not belong entirely to history. There is a vitality in "The Daughters of the Late Colonel" and "The Garden Party" and (with due respect to Virginia Woolf's strictures) "Bliss" that will outlast their historical importance. "At the Bay," "Prelude," and "The Stranger" will be read with approval by those who delight in an artistically controlled and verbally harmonious vision of reality. The same desire to get beneath the apparent ugliness of life to the hidden beauty that Mansfield gives voice to in her letters is occasionally satisfied in this short story or that. When it happens, the result more than justifies her hope that her stories may truly matter.

Notes

1—The Enigma of Katherine Mansfield

1. Antony Alpers, *Katherine Mansfield: A Biography* (New York: Alfred A. Knopf, 1954).

2. The chief sources of information on Mansfield's life are, in addition to Alpers's biography, these: *The Letters of Katherine Mansfield,* ed. J. Middleton Murry (New York: Alfred A. Knopf, 1932); *Katherine Mansfield's Letters to John Middleton Murry: 1913–1922* (New York: Alfred A. Knopf, 1951); John Middleton Murry, *The Autobiography of John Middleton Murry: Between Two Worlds* (New York: Julian Messner, 1936); *Journal of Katherine Mansfield: Definitive Edition,* ed. J. Middleton Murry (London: Constable & Co., 1962); and *The Scrapbook of Katherine Mansfield,* ed. J. Middleton Murry (New York: Alfred A. Knopf, 1940).

3. Stephen Hudson, "First Meeting with Katherine Mansfield," *Cornhill* 170 (Autumn 1958), p. 206.

4. *Katherine Mansfield's Letters to John Middleton Murry. 1913–1922,* p. 94. This book will be referred to hereafter as *Letters to . . . Murry.*

5. *Letters to . . . Murry,* p. 552.

6. The biographical details given below are drawn mainly from Antony Alpers's biography.

7. Katherine Mansfield, *The Short Stories of Katherine Mansfield* (New York: Alfred A. Knopf, 1937).

8. A. R. Orage, *Selected Essays and Critical Writings,* ed. Herbert Read and Denis Saurat (London: Stanley Nott, 1935), p. 125.

9. Ibid., pp. 130–31.

10. Katherine Mansfield, *In a German Pension* (London: Stephen Swift, 1911).

11. Sylvia Berkman, *Katherine Mansfield: A Critical Study* (London: Oxford University Press, 1951). This book was originally published by Yale University Press. Saralyn R. Daly, *Katherine Mansfield* (New York: Twayne Publishers, 1965).

2—*The Artist as Critic*

1. Katherine Mansfield, *Novels & Novelists*, ed. J. Middleton Murry (Boston: Beacon Press, 1959); the book was first published by Constable and Co. in 1930.

2. See *Katherine Mansfield's Letters to John Middleton Murry: 1913–1922*, ed. John Middleton Murry (New York: Alfred A. Knopf, 1951) for the years 1914–18.

3. *Novels & Novelists*, p. 84.

4. Ibid., p. 157.

5. Ibid., p. 48.

6. Ibid., p. 49.

7. *Letters to . . . Murry*, p. 380.

8. Ibid., p. 544.

9. In a letter to Dorothy Brett dated November 11, 1921, in *The Letters of Katherine Mansfield*, ed. John Middleton Murry (New York: Alfred A. Knopf, 1932), p. 416. Subsequent citations to this book will be to *Letters*.

10. *Novels & Novelists*, pp. 125–26.

11. Ibid., pp. 137, 140.

12. Ibid., p. 41.

13. *Letters to . . . Murry*, p. 544.

14. Ibid., p. 584.

15. *Novels & Novelists*, p. 308.

16. Ibid., p. 306.

17. Ibid., p. 19.

18. Ibid., p. 76.

19. Ibid., p. 109.

20. Ibid., p. 183.

21. *Letters*, p. 74.

22. *Novels & Novelists*, pp. 36–38.

23. Ibid., p. 30.

24. Ibid., p. 42.

25. Ibid., pp. 228–29, 252.

26. *Letters to . . . Murry,* p. 598.

27. *The Scrapbook of Katherine Mansfield,* ed. J. Middleton Murry (New York: Alfred A. Knopf, 1940), p. 233. Subsequent citations will be to the *Scrapbook.*

28. *Novels & Novelists,* p. 95.

29. Ibid., pp. 95–96.

30. Ibid., pp. 213–14.

31. Ibid., pp. 273–74.

32. *Letters,* p. 432. The letter is directed to Sydney Schiff on December 28, 1921.

33. *Letters,* p. 434, also to Schiff, dated January 15, 1922.

34. *Letters,* p. 464.

35. *Letters,* pp. 491–92.

36. *Scrapbook,* p. 245.

37. *Letters to . . . Murry,* p. 560.

38. *Letters,* p. 491.

39. *Novels & Novelists,* p. 308.

40. Ibid., p. 111.

41. The frequency with which Chekhov's work is mentioned in Murry's London *Athenaeum* during the years 1919–21 is directly attributable to his wife's enthusiasm for Chekhov as a human being, a writer of fiction, and a writer of letters.

42. *Journal of Katherine Mansfield: Definitive Edition,* ed. J. Middleton Murry (London: Constable & Co., 1962), pp. 226–27 passim. Subsequent citations will be to the *Journal.*

43. *Letters to . . . Murry,* p. 674.

44. *Letters,* pp. 194, 473.

45. 1919–21.

46. *Novels & Novelists,* pp. 304–6.

47. Ibid., pp. 246–47.

48. Ibid., pp. 38–40.

3—"Prelude" and "At the Bay"

1. *Journal of Katherine Mansfield: Definitive Edition,* ed. J. Middleton Murry (London: Constable & Co., 1962), p. 95.

2. Ibid.

3. Only in Sylvia Berkman's study is there an extended treatment that does justice to these stories. See also, Sam Hynes, "Katherine Mansfield: The Defeat of the Personal," *South Atlantic Quarterly* 52 (October 1953), pp. 555–60; George Shelton Hubbell, "Katherine Mansfield and Kezia," *Sewanee Review* 25 (July 1927), pp. 325–35; Celeste Turner Wright, "Katherine Mansfield's Boat Image," *Twentieth Century Literature* 1 (October 1955), pp. 128–32.

4. *The Letters of Katherine Mansfield*, ed. J. Middleton Murry (New York: Alfred A. Knopf, 1932), pp. 452–53.

5. Ibid., p. 182.

6. Ibid., p. 74.

7. *The Scrapbook of Katherine Mansfield*, ed. J Middleton Murry (New York: Alfred A. Knopf, 1940), p. 47.

8. *Letters*, p. 75.

9. Page references to Mansfield's longer stories will be cited in parentheses in the text.

10. In this respect, as in some others, she resembles Virginia Woolf's later creation, Mrs. Ramsay of *To the Lighthouse.*

11. Cf. Stephen Hudson, "First Meeting with Katherine Mansfield," *Cornhill* 170 (Autumn 1958), pp. 202–12.

12. See Chekhov's "Gooseberries" for an obvious treatment of this motif; and in Joyce's *Dubliners*, though almost any story in the volume will do, note particularly "Clay," "Araby," and "The Dead."

13. Cf. particularly Mansfield's *Scrapbook*, pp. 193–96. Ironically, though Mansfield's own husband was publishing studies of Keats, she felt that he was incapable of understanding her anguish as Fanny Brawne was Keats's.

14. Stein's terminology in Conrad's *Lord Jim.*

15. See chapter 5, pp. 77 ff and 112 ff.

16. Recall the description of Miss Kilman in *Mrs. Dalloway* and the motif of the man in the mackintosh in *Ulysses.*

17. *Letters*, pp. 400–401.

18. Ibid., p. 408.

19. *Journal*, pp. 267, 271.

20. For an excellent analysis of this story, see David Mad-

den, "Katherine Mansfield's 'Miss Brill,' " *University Review* 31 (December 1964), pp. 89–92.

21. Katherine Mansfield, *The Aloe* (New York: Alfred A. Knopf, 1930).

4–Man and Woman

1. Cf. *The Autobiography of John Middleton Murry: Between Two Worlds*, the letters of Mansfield to Murry, and Antony Alpers's *Katherine Mansfield: A Biography* for an understanding of the complicated emotional relationship.

2. *Katherine Mansfield's Letters to John Middleton Murry: 1913–1922*, ed. John Middleton Murry (New York: Alfred A. Knopf, 1951), p. 158.

3. Ibid., p. 105.

4. Ibid., p. 116.

5. Ibid., p. 141.

6. Ibid., p. 155.

7. Ibid., p. 182.

8. Ibid., p. 84.

9. Ibid., p. 275.

10. Ibid., p. 208.

11. Antony Alpers, *Katherine Mansfield: A Biography* (New York: Alfred A. Knopf, 1954), p. 162 ff.

12. *The Scrapbook of Katherine Mansfield*, ed. J. Middleton Murry (New York: Alfred A. Knopf, 1940), pp. 147–48.

13. John Middleton Murry, *The Autobiography of John Middleton Murry: Between Two Worlds* (New York: Julian Messner, 1936), p. 205.

14. Ibid., pp. 206–7.

15. Ibid., p. 463.

16. Ibid., p. 465.

17. *Letters to . . . Murry*, p. 151.

18. *Autobiography of John Middleton Murry*, p. 464.

19. *Letters to . . . Murry*, p. 149.

20. Ibid., p. 148 passim.

21. *Scrapbook*, pp. 145–47.

22. *Letters to . . . Murry*, p. 266.

23. Ibid.

5–The Legacy of Fiction

1. Saralyn R. Daly, *Katherine Mansfield* (New York: Twayne Publishers, 1965), pp. 80–88.

2. *Katherine Mansfield's Letters to John Middleton Murry: 1913–1922*, ed. John Middleton Murry (New York: Alfred A. Knopf, 1951), p. 211.

3. Cf. Katherine Mansfield, *Novels & Novelists*, ed. J. Middleton Murry (Boston: Beacon Press, 1959).

4. *The Short Stories of Katherine Mansfield* (New York: Alfred A. Knopf, 1937), p. 260.

5. *Letters to . . . Murry*, p. 94.

6. In a letter dated March 22, 1915, Mansfield reports to Murry that "at B's this afternoon there arrived 'du monde,' including a very lovely young woman, married and *curious*—blonde—passionate. We danced together." (*Letters to . . . Murry*, p. 23). The definitive edition of Mansfield's *Journal* (London, 1954) describes a lesbian relationship between Mansfield and a young woman in 1907 (pp. 12–13).

7. *Letters to . . . Murry*, p. 189.

8. That the dinner party may be a love feast as well is suggested by a line in Mansfield's letter to Murry dated May 22, 1918. Exhorting him to "eat fruit while the warm weather lasts—and remember what you are to me," she continues: "My love seems all to be expressed in terms of food." *Letters to . . . Murry*, p. 257.

9. Frank Swinnerton, *Figures in the Foreground: Literary Reminiscences, 1917–1940* (London, 1963), pp. 59–60.

10. *The Letters of Katherine Mansfield*, ed. J. Middleton Murry (New York: Alfred A. Knopf, 1932), p. 205.

11. Ibid., p. 359.

12. Ibid., pp. 388–89.

13. In "A Rose for Emily."

14. *Journal of Katherine Mansfield: Definitive Edition*, ed. J. Middleton Murry (London: Constable & Co., 1962), p. 281.

15. Joyce's "The Sisters."

16. *Letters*, p. 389.

17. *Letters to . . . Murry*, p. 597.

18. See the treatment of this story by Saralyn Daly in *Katherine Mansfield*, pp. 102–6, and by Sylvia Berkman in *Katherine Mansfield: A Critical Study* (New Haven, Conn.: Yale University Press, 1951), pp. 165–67.

19. Antony Alpers, *Katherine Mansfield: A Biography* (New York: Alfred A. Knopf, 1954), p. 305.

20. *Journal*, pp. 123–24.

21. *Letters*, p. 454.

22. A. R. Orage, *Selected Essays and Critical Writings*, ed. Herbert Read and Denis Saurat (London: Stanley Nott, 1935), p. 129. Orage reports Mansfield as having told him: "I've been a camera. . . . a selective camera, and it has been my attitude that has determined the selection; with the result that my slices of life . . . have been partial, misleading, and a little malicious."

23. Mansfield's concern with the implications of the garden image is expressed in a letter to William Gerhardi (*Letters*, p. 449): "*And* the reason why I used the 'florid' image was that I was writing about a garden party. It seemed natural that the day should close like a flower. People had been looking at flowers all the afternoon, you see."

24. James Joyce, "Ibsen's New Drama," *The Critical Writings*, eds. Ellsworth Mason and Richard Ellmann (New York: Viking, 1959).

25. In a letter to Richard Murry dated January 17, 1921 (*Letters*, pp. 360–61), Mansfield says: "It's a very queer thing how *craft* comes into writing. . . . *Par example.* In "Miss Brill" I choose not only the length of every sentence, but even the sound of every sentence. I choose the rise and fall of every paragraph to fit her. . . ."

26. *Journal*, p. 266.

27. *The Scrapbook of Katherine Mansfield*, ed. J. Middleton Murry (New York: Alfred A. Knopf, 1932), especially pp. 209–14.

28. For interesting critical views of "The Garden Party," see Don W. Kleine, " 'The Garden Party': A Portrait of the Artist," *Criticism* 5 (Fall 1963), pp. 360–71; Donald S. Taylor and Daniel A. Weiss, "Crashing the Garden Party," *Modern Fiction Studies* 4 (Winter 1958–59), pp. 361–64;

Warren Walker, "The Unresolved Conflict in 'The Garden Party,'" *Modern Fiction Studies* 3 (Winter 1957–58), pp. 354–58; and Robert Murray Davis, "The Unity of 'The Garden Party,'" *Studies in Short Fiction* 2 (Fall 1964), pp. 61–65.

6–Katherine Mansfield: The Summing Up

1. Virginia Woolf, *A Writer's Diary: Being Extracts from the Diary of Virginia Woolf,* ed. Leonard Woolf (London: Hogarth Press, 1965, p. 2.

2. Ibid., p. 329.

3. Cf. the stories of Katherine Mansfield's *In a German Pension* (London: Stephen Swift, 1911) and "The Lady's Maid," "The Little Governess," and "Je ne parle pas français."

4. "M. B. Oxon," *Cosmic Anatomy, or the Structure of the Ego* (London: Watkins, 1921).

5. *Katherine Mansfield's Letters to John Middleton Murry: 1913–1922,* ed. John Middleton Murry (New York: Alfred A. Knopf, 1951), p. 2.

6. Ibid., p. 603.

7. Ibid., p. 569.

8. Cf. Katherine Mansfield, *Novels & Novelists,* ed. by J. Middleton Murry (Boston: Beacon Press, 1959).

9. R. W. Stallman, "Mansfield's 'The Fly,'" *Explicator,* Item #49 (April 1945); and on the same subject, Willis D. Jacobs, *Explicator,* Item #32 (February 1947); Thomas Bledsoe, *Explicator,* Item #53 (May 1947); Celeste Turner Wright, "Genesis of a Short Story," *Philological Quarterly* 34 (January 1955), pp. 91–96; Pauline P. Bell, *Explicator,* Item #20 (December 1960); J. D. Thomas, "Symbol and Parallelism in 'The Fly,'" *College English* 22 (January 1961), pp. 256–62; and John T. Hagopian, "Capturing Mansfield's 'Fly,'" *Modern Fiction Studies* 9 (Winter 1963–64), pp. 385–90. The reply to Hagopian's article is by Ted E. Boyle, "The Death of the Boss: Another Look at Katherine Mansfield's 'The Fly,'" *Modern Fiction Studies* 11 (Summer 1965), pp. 183–85.

Selected Bibliography

Works by Katherine Mansfield

COLLECTED FICTION AND POETRY

The Aloe. New York: Alfred A. Knopf, 1930.

Bliss and Other Stories. London: Constable & Co., 1920.

The Dove's Nest and Other Stories. London: Constable & Co., 1923.

The Garden Party and Other Stories. London: Constable & Co., 1922.

In a German Pension. London: Stephen Swift, 1911.

The Little Girl and Other Stories. New York: Alfred A. Knopf, 1924.

Poems. London: Constable & Co., 1923.

The Short Stories of Katherine Mansfield. New York: Alfred A. Knopf, 1937.

NONFICTION COLLECTIONS

Journal of Katherine Mansfield: Definitive Edition, Ed. J. Middleton Murry. London: Constable & Co., 1962.

Katherine Mansfield's Letters to John Middleton Murry: 1913–1922, Ed. John Middleton Murry. New York: Alfred A. Knopf, 1951.

The Letters of Katherine Mansfield. Ed. J. Middleton Murry. New York: Alfred A. Knopf, 1932 (special one volume edition).

Novels & Novelists. Ed. J. Middleton Murry. Boston: Beacon Press, 1959.

The Scrapbook of Katherine Mansfield. Ed. J. Middleton Murry. New York: Alfred A. Knopf, 1940.

ARTICLES AND REVIEWS

The Adelphi: Vol. 1 (June 1923–May 1924); Vol. 2 (June 1924–May 1925).

The Athenaeum: contributions to this periodical are included in *Novels & Novelists,* cited above.

The Blue Review: Vol. 1 (May–July 1913).

The New Age: N. S. Vol. 6, 7, 9, 10, 18, 21 (1910–17).

Rhythm: Vols. 1–2 (Summer 1911–March 1913).

The Signature: Vol. 1 (October 4–November 1, 1915).

Works on Katherine Mansfield

BOOKS

Alpers, Antony. *Katherine Mansfield: A Biography.* New York: Alfred A. Knopf, 1954.

Beauchamp, Sir Harold. *Reminiscences and Recollections.* New Plymouth, New Zealand: T. Avery, 1937.

Berkman, Sylvia. *Katherine Mansfield: A Critical Study.* New Haven, Conn.: Yale University Press, 1951.

Bowen, Elizabeth. "Introduction," in *Stories by Katherine Mansfield,* ed. by Elizabeth Bowen. New York: Alfred A. Knopf, Vintage Books, 1956.

Cather, Willa. *On Writing: Critical Studies on Writing as an Art.* New York: Alfred A. Knopf, 1949.

Daiches, David. *New Literary Values.* Edinburgh: Oliver and Boyd, 1936.

———. *The Novel and the Modern World.* Chicago: University of Chicago Press, 1939.

Daly, Saralyn R. *Katherine Mansfield.* New York: Twayne Publishers, 1965.

Gordon, Ian A. *Katherine Mansfield.* London: Longmans, Green & Co., 1954.

Hastings, Beatrice. *The Old "New Age": Orage and Others.* London: Blue Moon Press, 1936.

Hormasji, Nariman. *Katherine Mansfield: An Appraisal.* London: William Collins Sons & Co., 1967.

Lawrence, D. H. *The Letters of D. H. Lawrence.* Edited and

with an introduction by Aldous Huxley. London: William Heinemann, 1956.

Lea, F. A. *The Life of John Middleton Murry.* New York: Oxford University Press, 1960.

Mantz, Ruth Elvish. *The Critical Bibliography of Katherine Mansfield.* London: Constable & Co., 1931.

Mantz, Ruth Elvish and J. Middleton Murry. *The Life of Katherine Mansfield.* London: Constable & Co., 1933.

Murry, John Middleton. *The Autobiography of John Middleton Murry: Between Two Worlds.* New York: Julian Messner, 1936.

———. *Katherine Mansfield and Other Literary Portraits.* London: Peter Nevill, 1949.

Orage, A. R. *Selected Essays and Critical Writings.* Eds. Herbert Read and Denis Saurat. London: Stanley Nott, 1935.

Swinnerton, Frank. *Figures in the Foreground: Literary Reminiscences, 1917–1940.* London: Hutchinson, 1963.

Woolf, Virginia. *A Writer's Diary: Being Extracts from the Diary of Virginia Woolf.* Ed. Leonard Woolf. London: Hogarth Press, 1965.

SELECTED ARTICLES ON KATHERINE MANSFIELD

Armstrong, Martin. "The Art of Katherine Mansfield," *Fortnightly Review,* N. S. 113 (March 1923), pp. 484–90.

Bell, Pauline P. "Mansfield's 'The Fly,'" *Explicator,* Item #20 (December 1960).

Bledsoe, Thomas. "Mansfield's 'The Fly,'" *Explicator,* Item #53 (May 1947).

Boyle, Ted E. "The Death of the Boss: Another Look at Katherine Mansfield's 'The Fly,'" *Modern Fiction Studies* 11 (Summer 1965), pp. 183–85.

Cox, Sidney. "The Fastidiousness of Katherine Mansfield," *Sewanee Review* 34 (April–June 1931), pp. 158–69.

Davis, Robert Murray. "The Unity of 'The Garden Party,'" *Studies in Short Fiction* 2 (Fall 1964) pp. 61–65.

Eisinger, Chester. "Mansfield's 'Bliss,'" *Explicator,* Item #48 (May 1949).

Freeman, Kathleen. "The Art of Katherine Mansfield," *The Canadian Forum* 7 (July 1927), pp. 302–7.

Gargano, James. "Mansfield's 'Miss Brill,'" *Explicator*, Item #10 (November 1960).

Garlington, Jack. "Katherine Mansfield: The Critical Trend," *Twentieth-Century Literature* 2 (July 1956), pp. 51–61.

———. "An Unattributed Story by Katherine Mansfield?" *Modern Language Notes* 71 (February 1956), pp. 91–93.

Greenfield, Stanley. "Mansfield's 'The Fly,'" *Explicator*, Item #2 (October 1958).

Hagopian, John T. "Capturing Mansfield's 'Fly,'" *Modern Fiction Studies* 9 (Winter 1963–64), pp. 385–90).

Hubbell, George Shelton. "Katherine Mansfield and Kezia," *Sewanee Review* 25 (July 1927), pp. 325–35.

Hudson, Stephen. "First Meetings with Katherine Mansfield," *Cornhill* 170 (Autumn 1958), pp. 202–12.

Hynes, Sam. "Katherine Mansfield: The Defeat of the Personal," *South Atlantic Quarterly* 52 (October 1953), pp. 555–60.

Jacobs, Willis D. "Mansfield's 'The Fly,'" *Explicator*, Item #32 (February 1947).

Kleine, Don W. "The Chekhovian Source of 'Marriage à la Mode,'" *Philological Quarterly* 42 (April 1963), pp. 284–88.

———. "'The Garden Party': A Portrait of the Artist," *Criticism* 5 (Fall 1963), pp. 360–71.

———. "Katherine Mansfield and the Prisoner of Love," *Criticism* 3 (1961), pp. 20–33.

Madden, David. "Katherine Mansfield's 'Miss Brill,'" *University Review* (Kansas City) 31 (December 1964), pp. 88–92.

Porter, Katherine Anne. "The Art of Katherine Mansfield," *Nation* 145 (October 23, 1937), pp. 435–36.

Pritchett, V. S. "Books in General," *New Statesman and Nation* 31 (February 2, 1946), p. 87.

Schneider, Elisabeth. "Katherine Mansfield and Chekhov," *Modern Language Notes* 50 (June 1935), pp. 394–97.

Sewell, Arthur. *Katherine Mansfield: A Critical Essay*, Aukland, New Zealand: Unicorn Press, 1936.

Shanks, Edward. "Katherine Mansfield," *London Mercury* 17 (January 1928), pp. 286–93.

Stallman, R. W. "Mansfield's 'The Fly,' " *Explicator*, Item #49 (April 1945).

Stanley, C. W. "The Art of Katherine Mansfield," *Dalhousie Review* 10 (April 1930), pp. 26–41.

Street, G. S. "Nos et Mutamur," *London Mercury* 5 (November 1921), pp. 55–57.

Taylor, Donald S. and Daniel A. Weiss. "Crashing the Garden Party," *Modern Fiction Studies* 4 (Winter 1958–59), pp. 361–64.

Thomas, J. D. "Symbol and Parallelism in 'The Fly,' " *College English* 22 (January 1961), pp. 256–62.

Van Kranendonk, A. G. "Katherine Mansfield," *English Studies* 12 (April 1930), pp. 49–57.

Wagenknecht, Edward. "Katherine Mansfield," *English Journal* 17 (April 1928), pp. 272–84.

Walker, Warren. "The Unresolved Conflict in 'The Garden Party,' " *Modern Fiction Studies* 3 (Winter 1957–58), pp. 354–58.

Whitridge, Arnold. "Katherine Mansfield," *Sewanee Review* 48 (April–June 1940), pp. 256–72.

Wright, Celeste Turner. "Darkness as a Symbol in Katherine Mansfield," *Modern Philology* 51 (February 1954), pp. 204–07.

———. "Genesis of a Short Story," *Philological Quarterly*, 34 (January 1955), pp. 91–96.

———. "Katherine Mansfield's Boat Image," *Twentieth-Century Literature* 1 (October 1955), pp. 128–32.

———. "Katherine Mansfield's Dog Image," *Literature and Psychology* 10 (Summer 1960), pp. 80–81.

———. "Mansfield's 'The Fly,' " *Explicator*, Item #27 (February 1954).

Index